Trento Colouring Book

It is well documented that, for many people (adults and children alike), colouring is a therapeutic, stress-relieving pastime.

What could be better, then, than colouring in images of the beautiful city of Trento in northern Italy? The typical Italian architecture makes a great subject for a colouring book.

Unlike most other colouring books which are usually filled with whimsical and cartoon images, mine are full of real pictures.

In this case, the colouring pages were created from photographs I took during a content creators' conference in Trento. You will find street scenes with impressive town houses painted in lovely pastel colours alongside pictures of the stunning Buonconsiglio Castle which dominates the Trento skyline. There are also images of beautiful tiled rooftops and church spires viewed from the castle's terrace. Piazza Duomo with its cathedral and incredible statue of Neptune features within these pages, as does the verdant park in front of the town's train station, complete with its statue of a typical Trento family. There are also photos of the bishop's palace, a statue of S. Vigilio, the patron saint of Trento, and some of the gorgeous flower gardens found in the city.

Grab your favourite pens or pencils and let your imagination and creativity run riot. I use high quality fine-tip felt pens for the details, and coloured pencils for the larger areas, but the choice is yours. Some people like to put a water colour wash across the whole picture before they begin. It's your creation. It's up to you!

Cut out your finished work and display it somewhere as in inspiration to travel further for longer, or as a reminder of places you've already been to.

Keep in touch with me at Happy Days Travel Blog or on social media:

@happydaystravelblog

@happydayswriter

Show me your creations, follow my travels and tell me about yours!

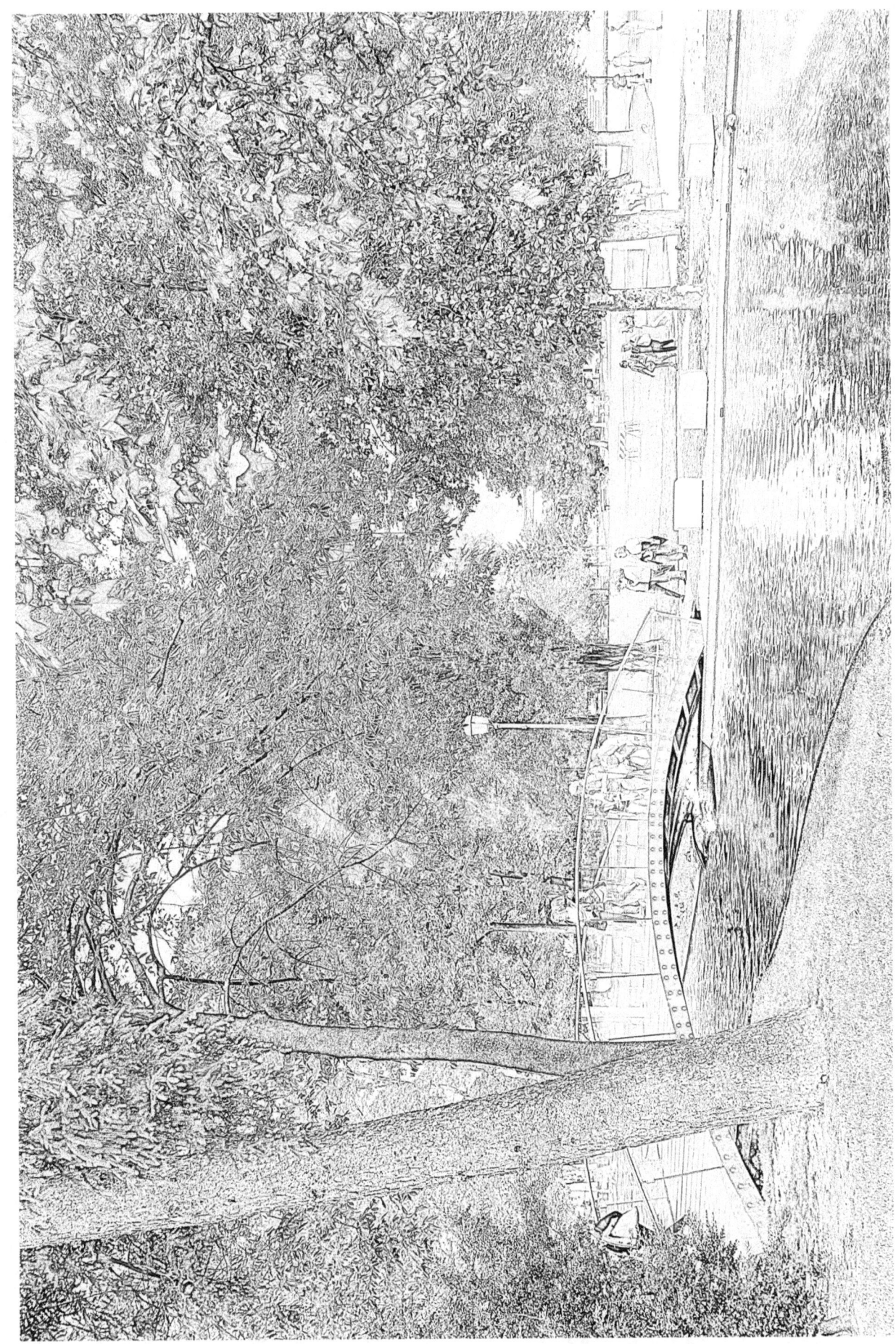

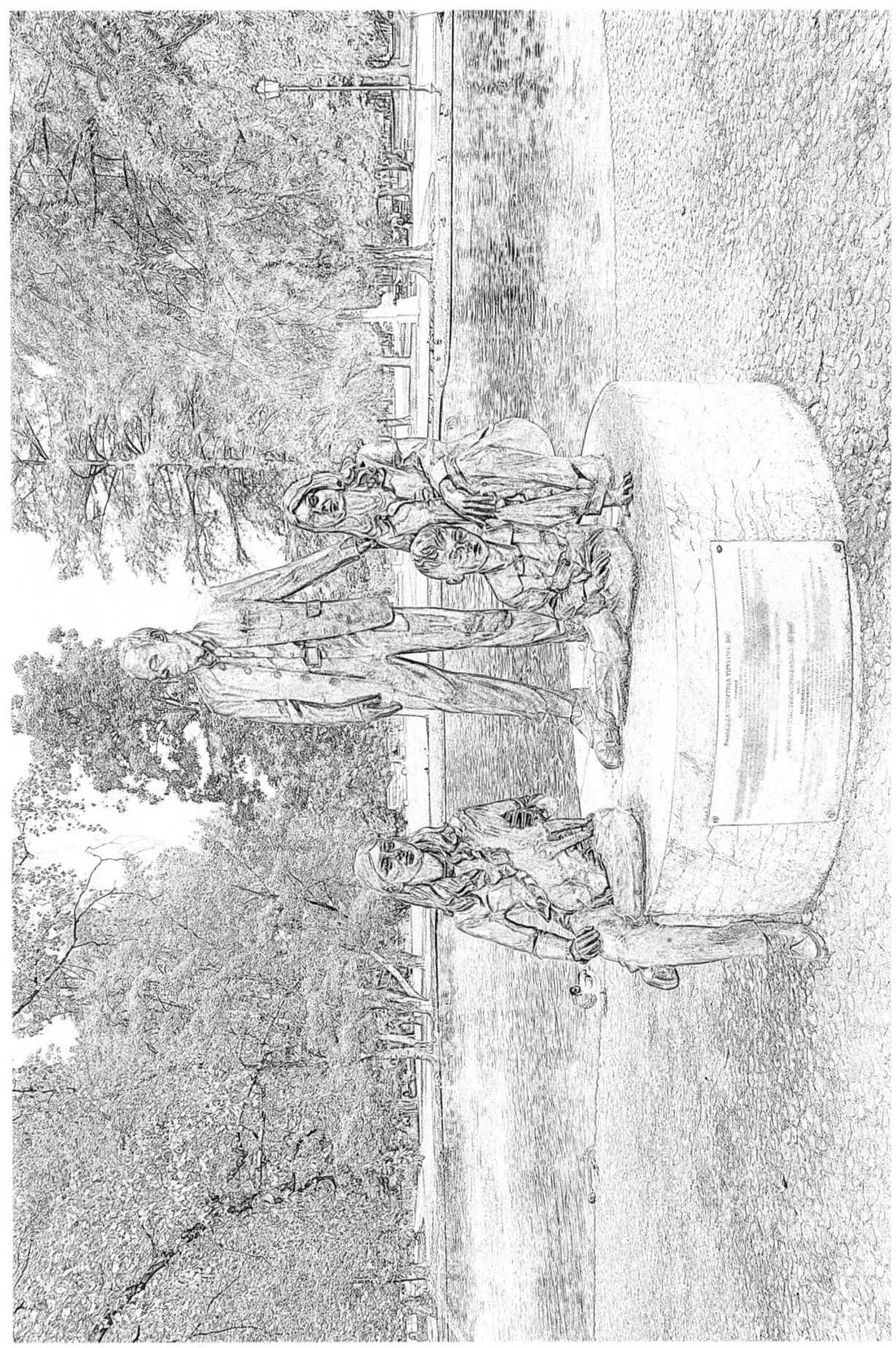

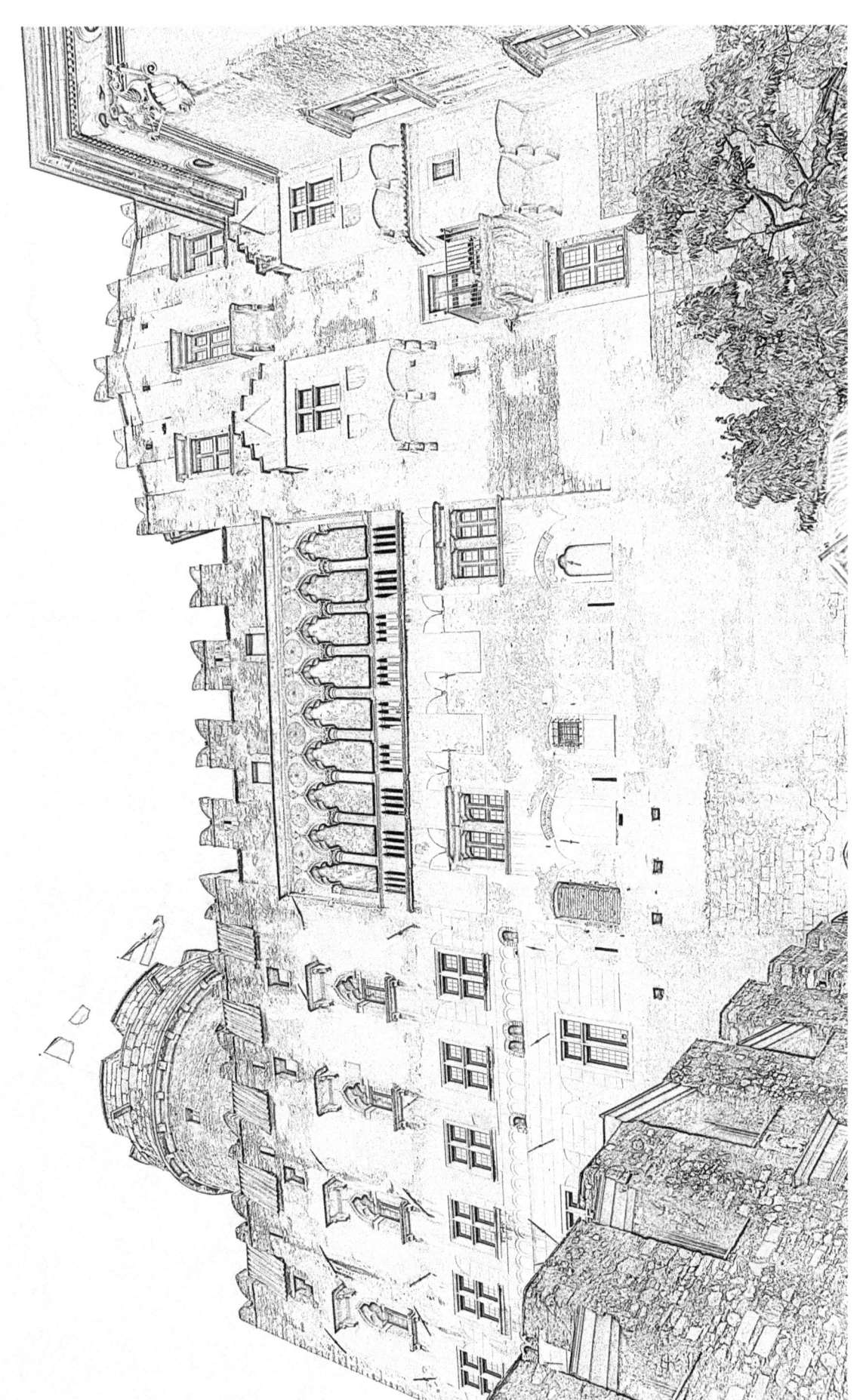

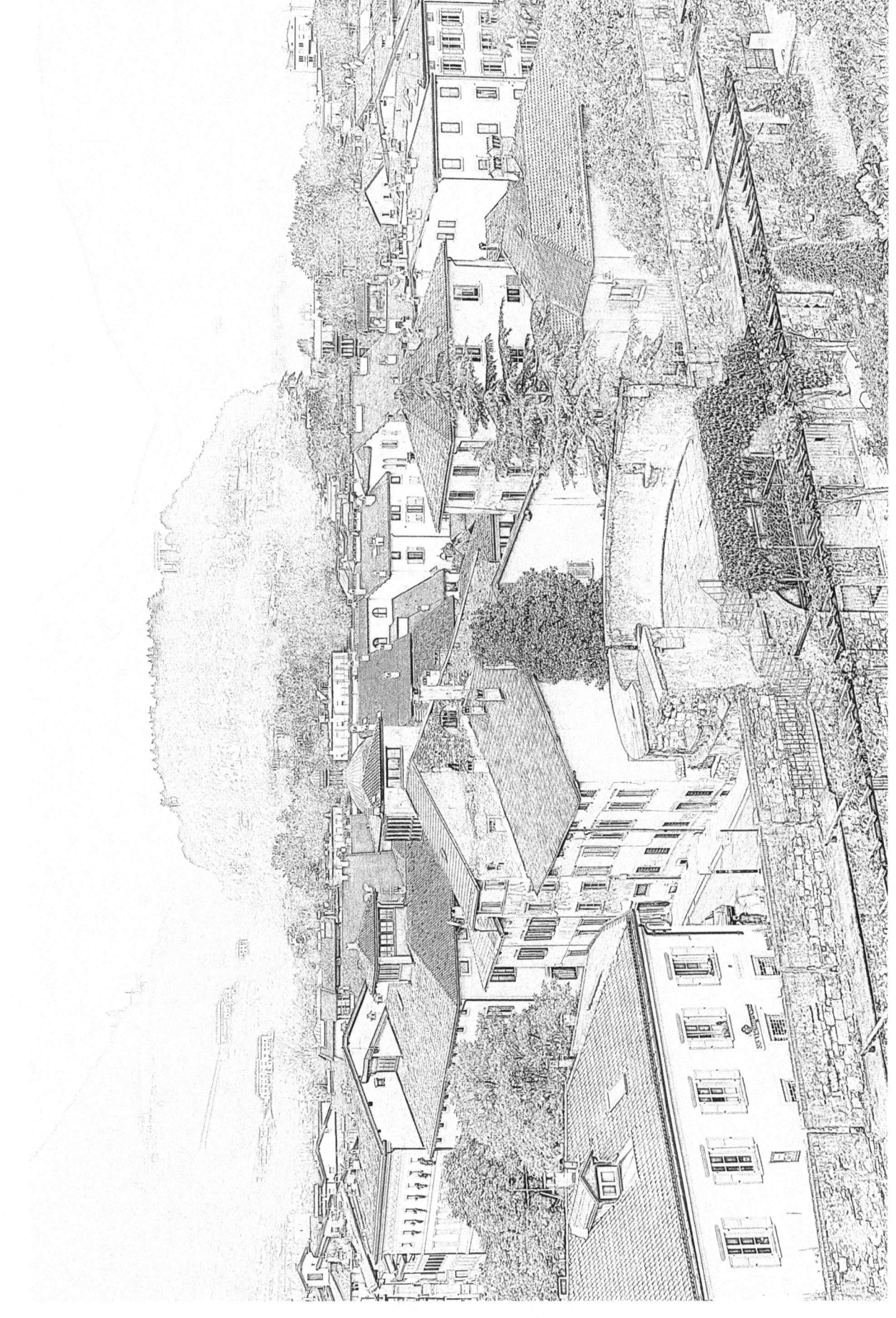

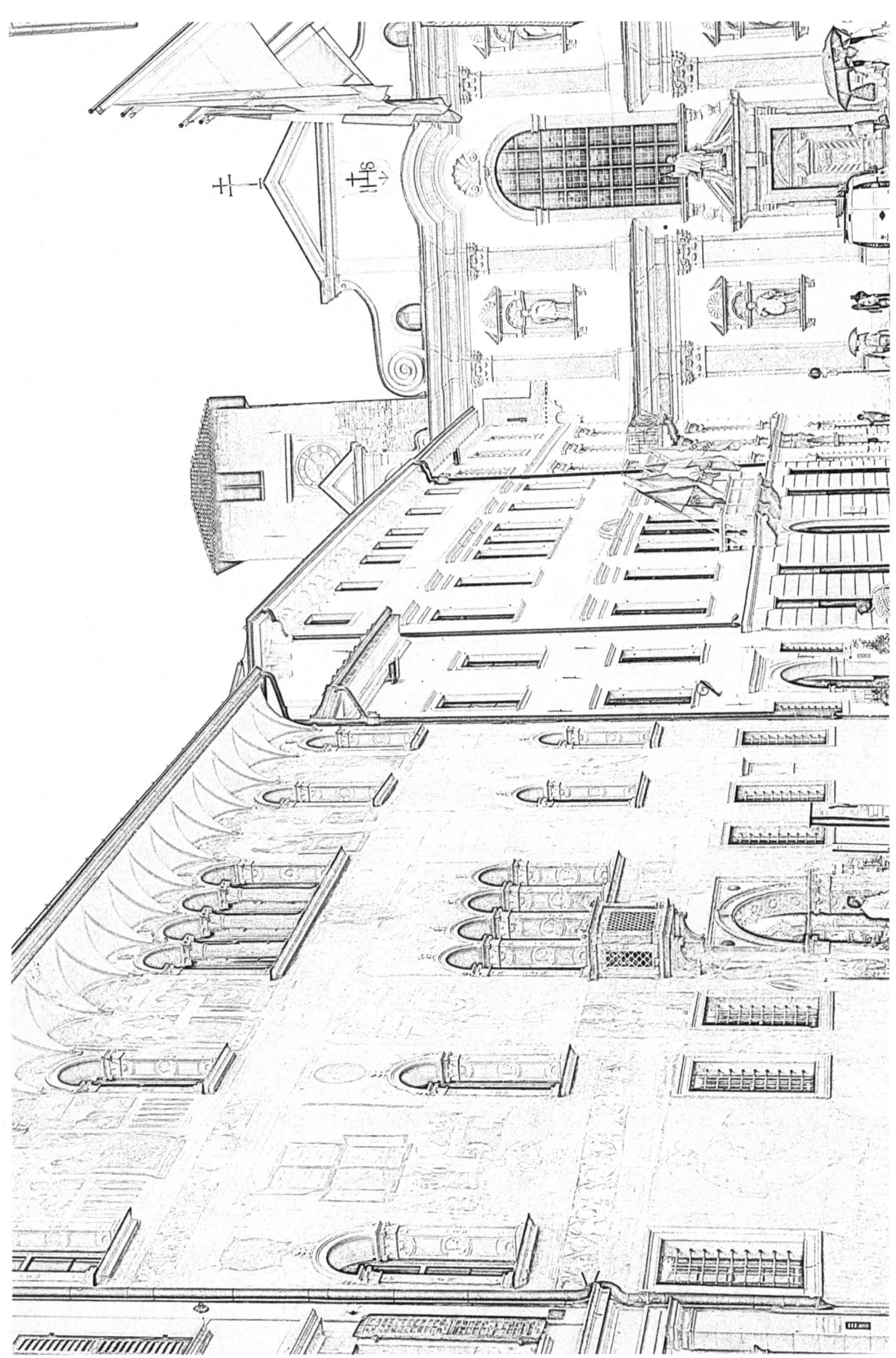

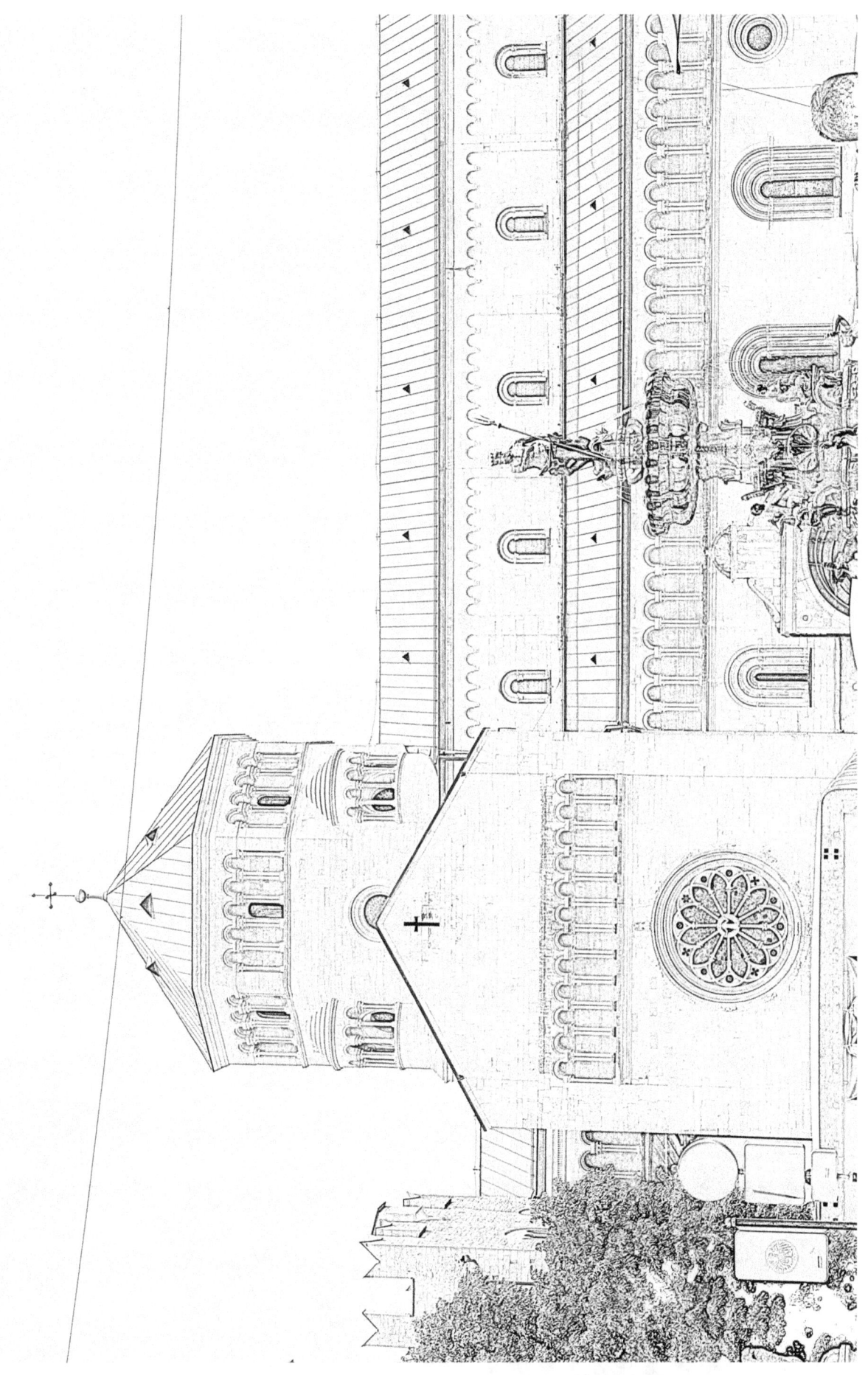

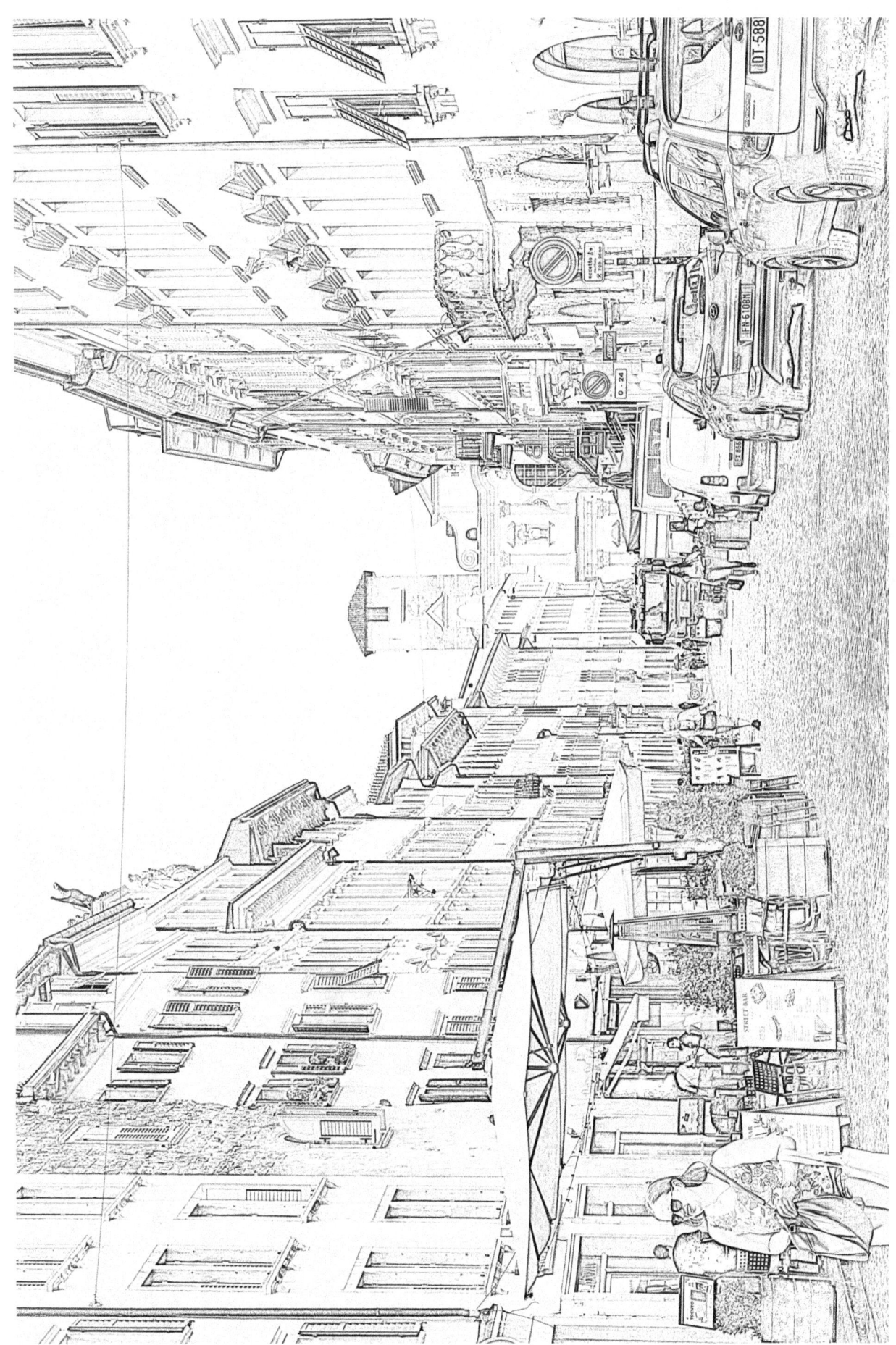

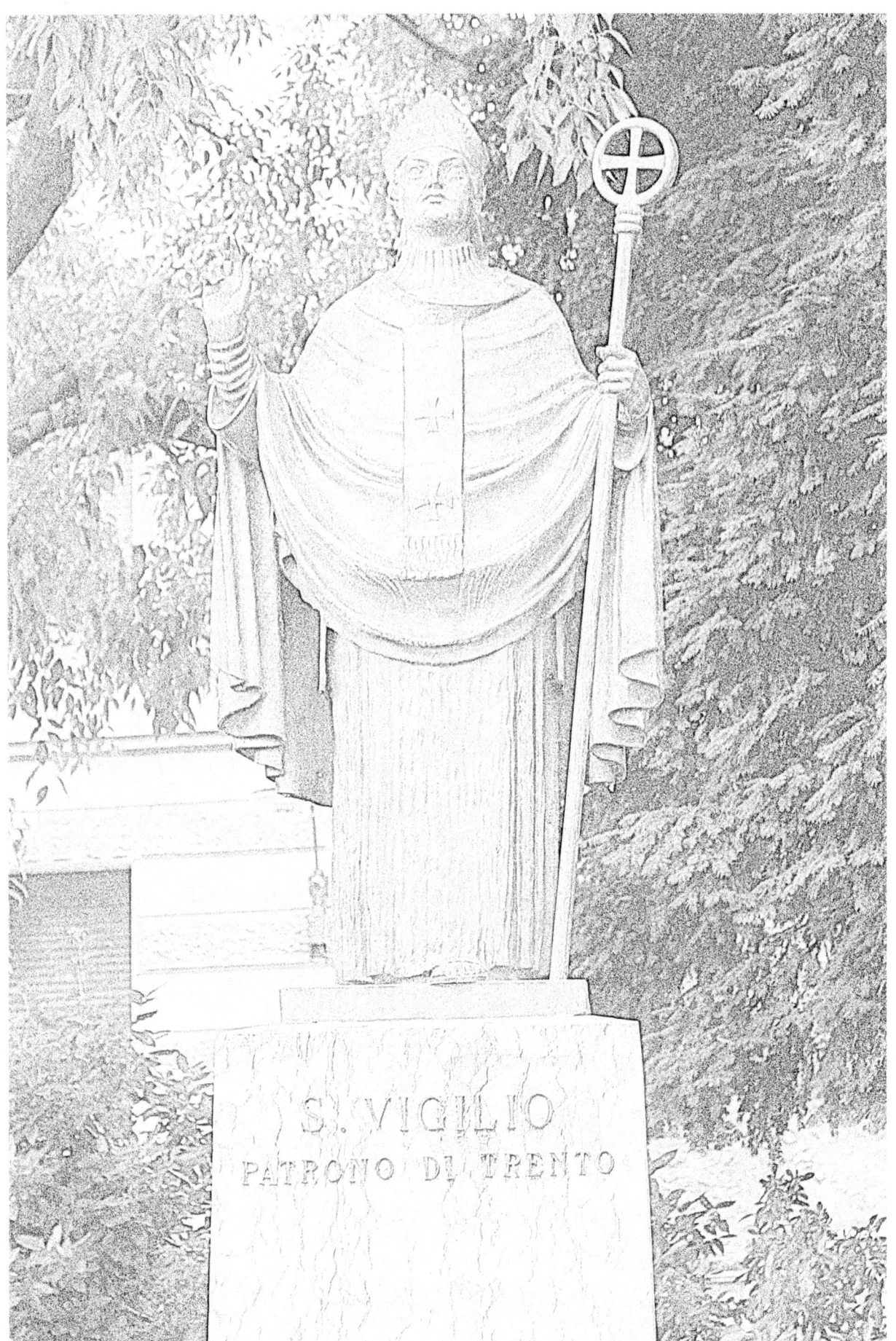

S. VIGILIO
PATRONO DI TRENTO

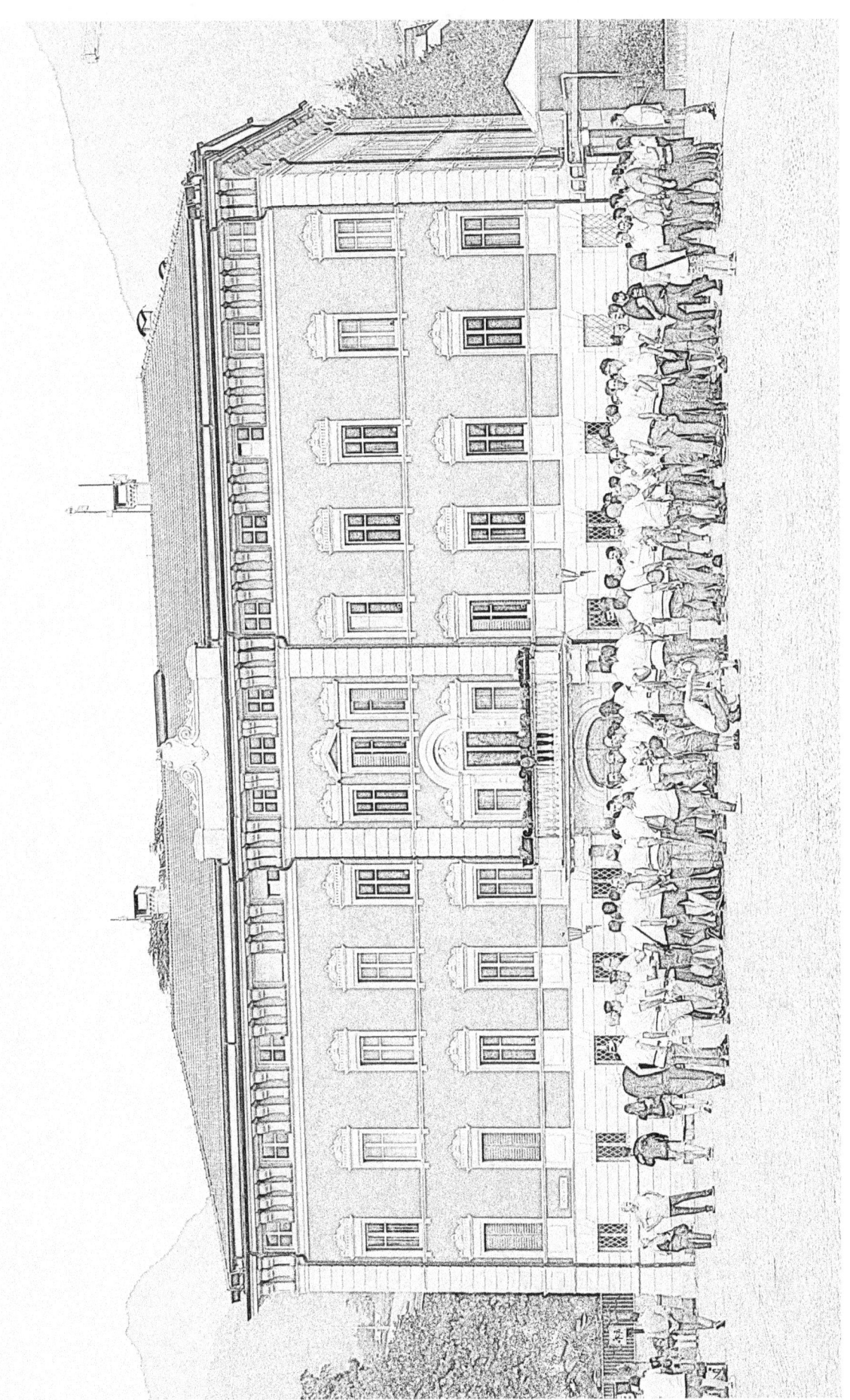

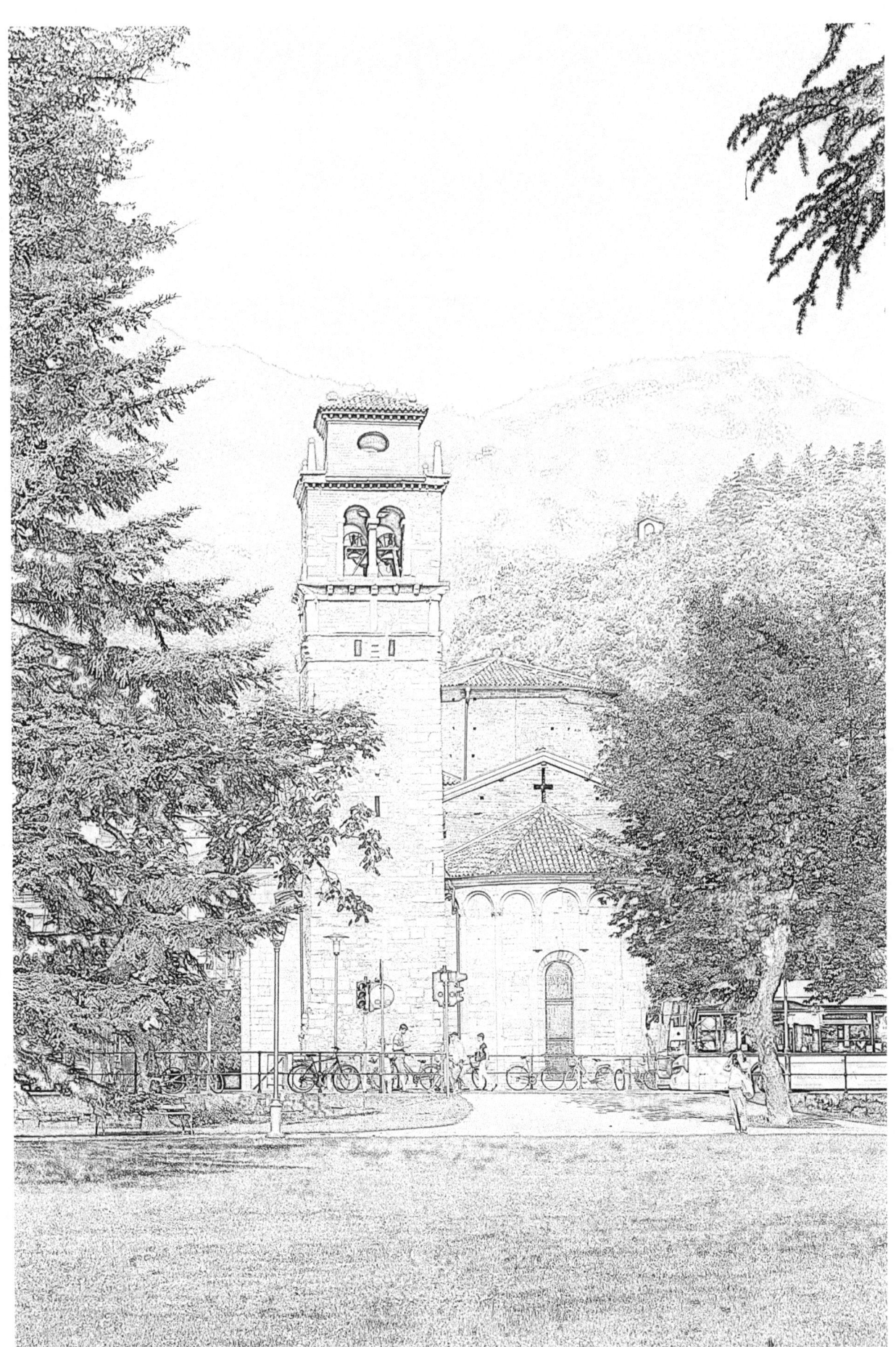

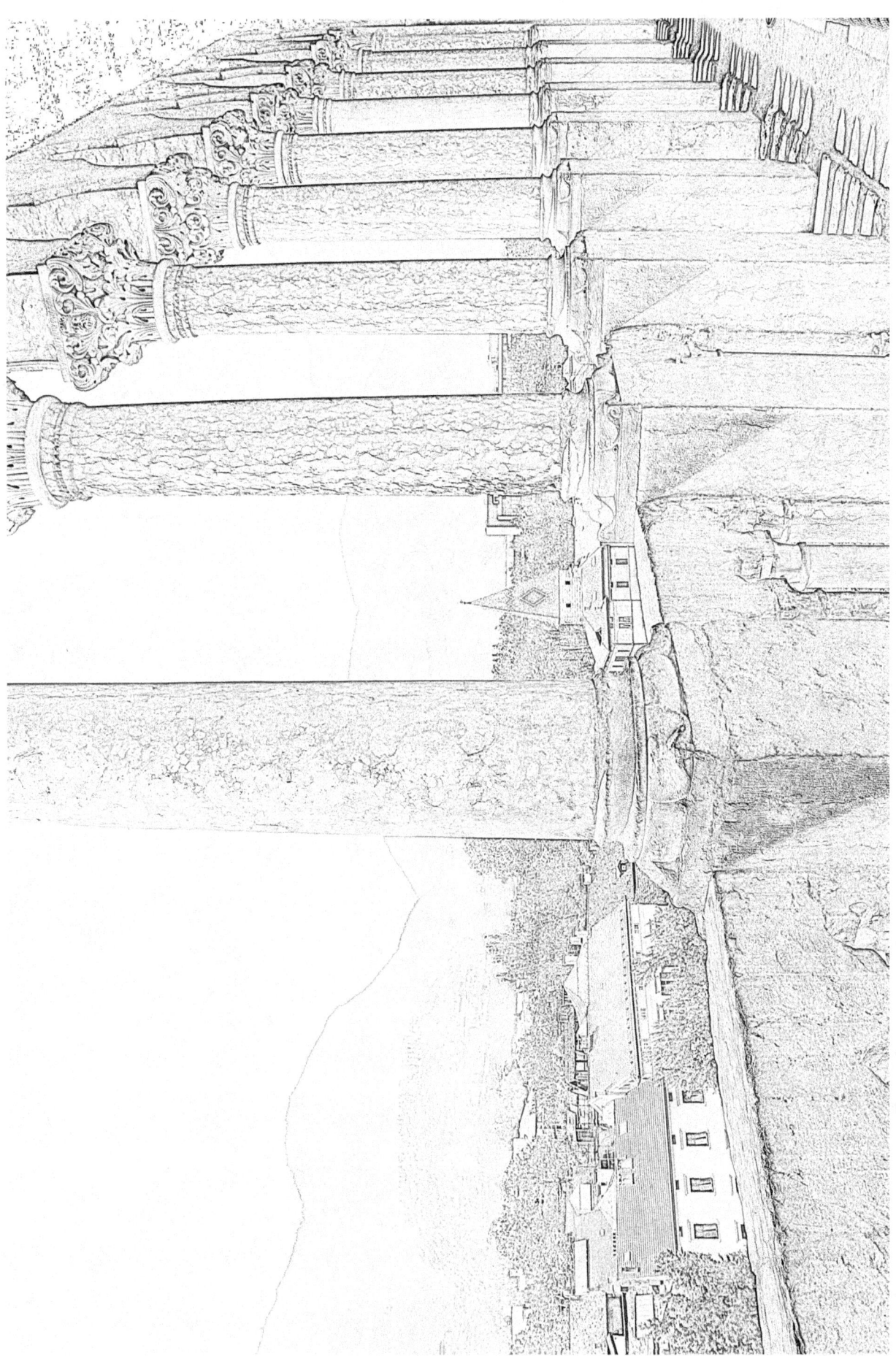

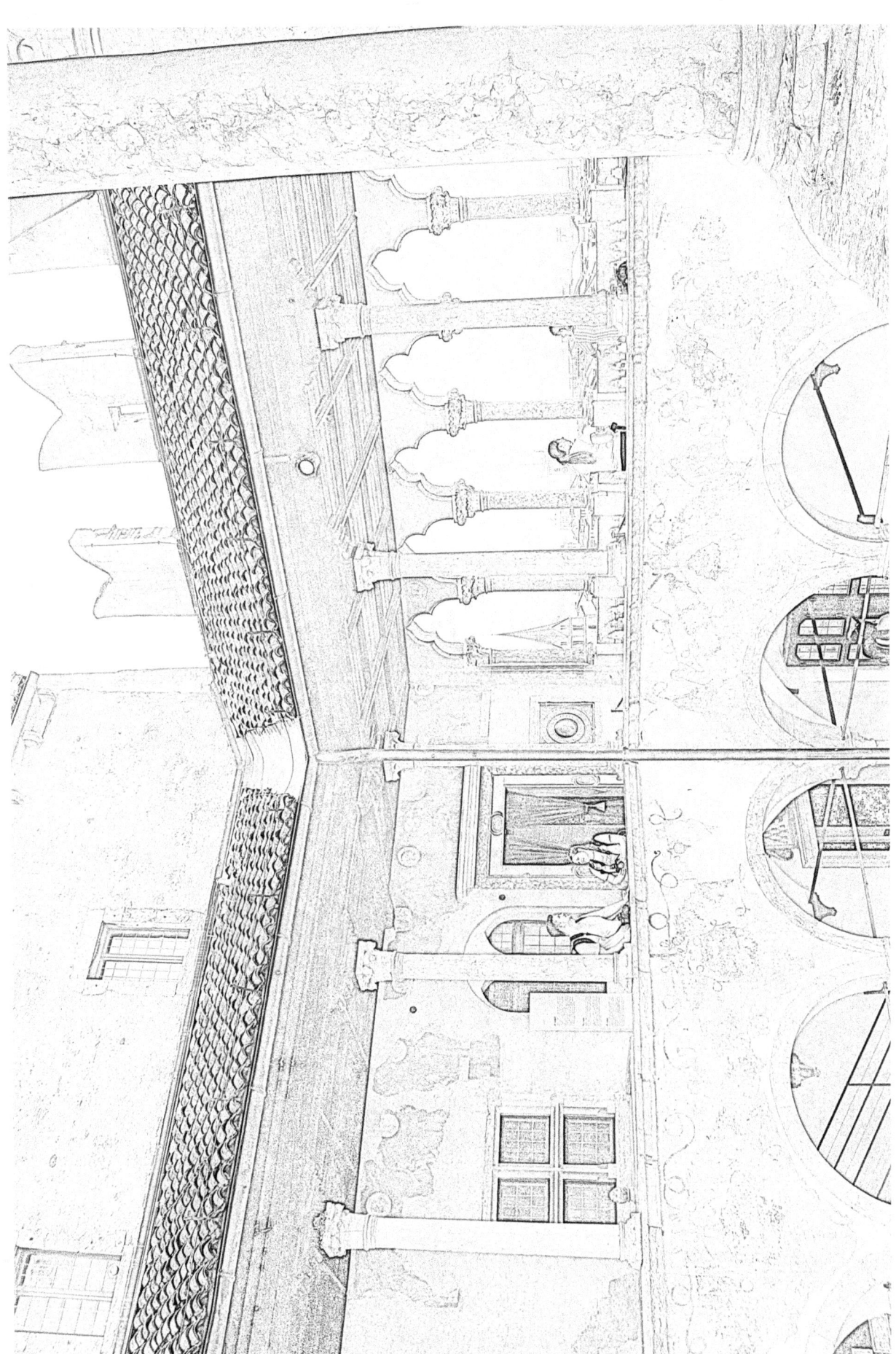

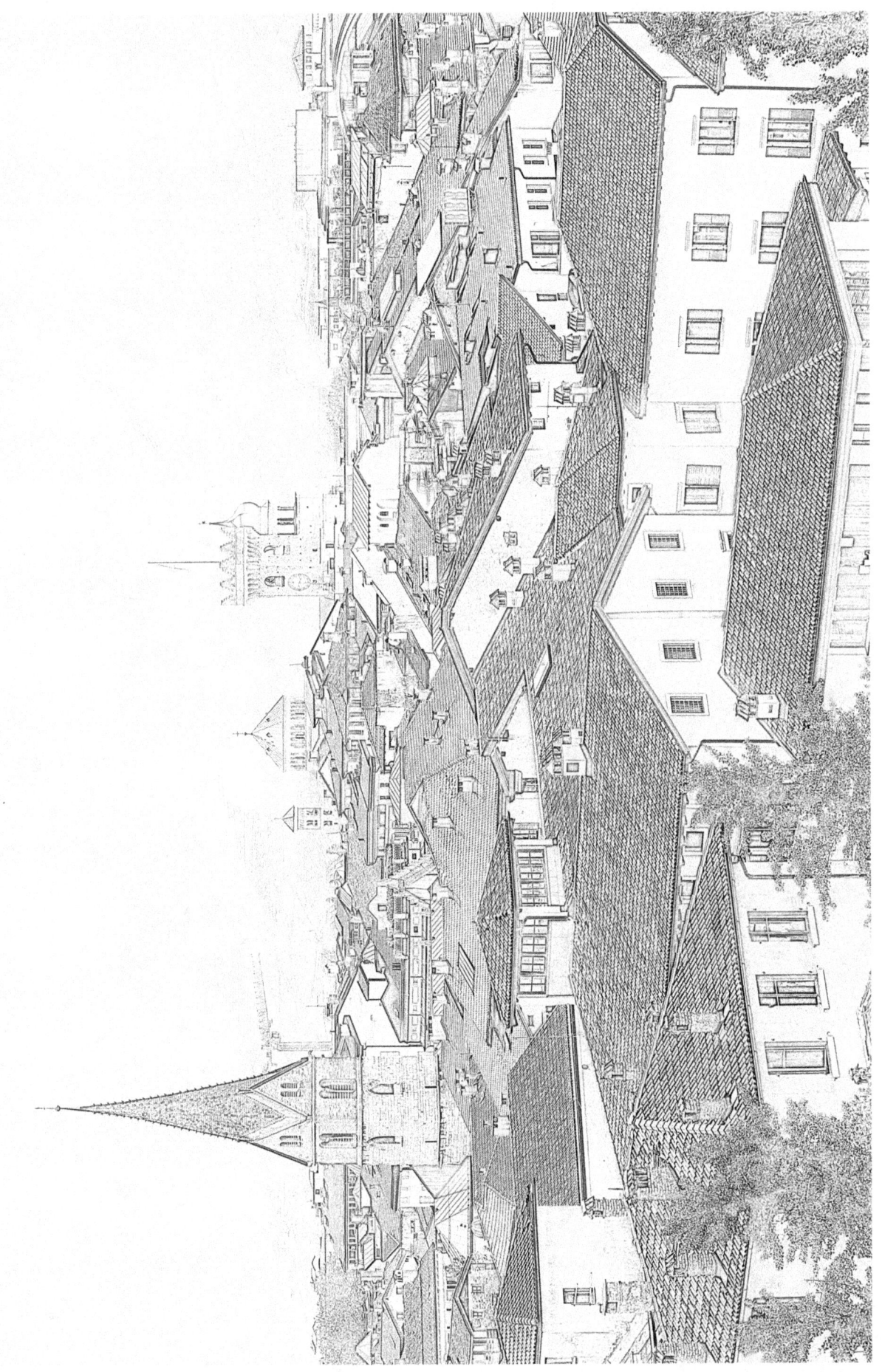

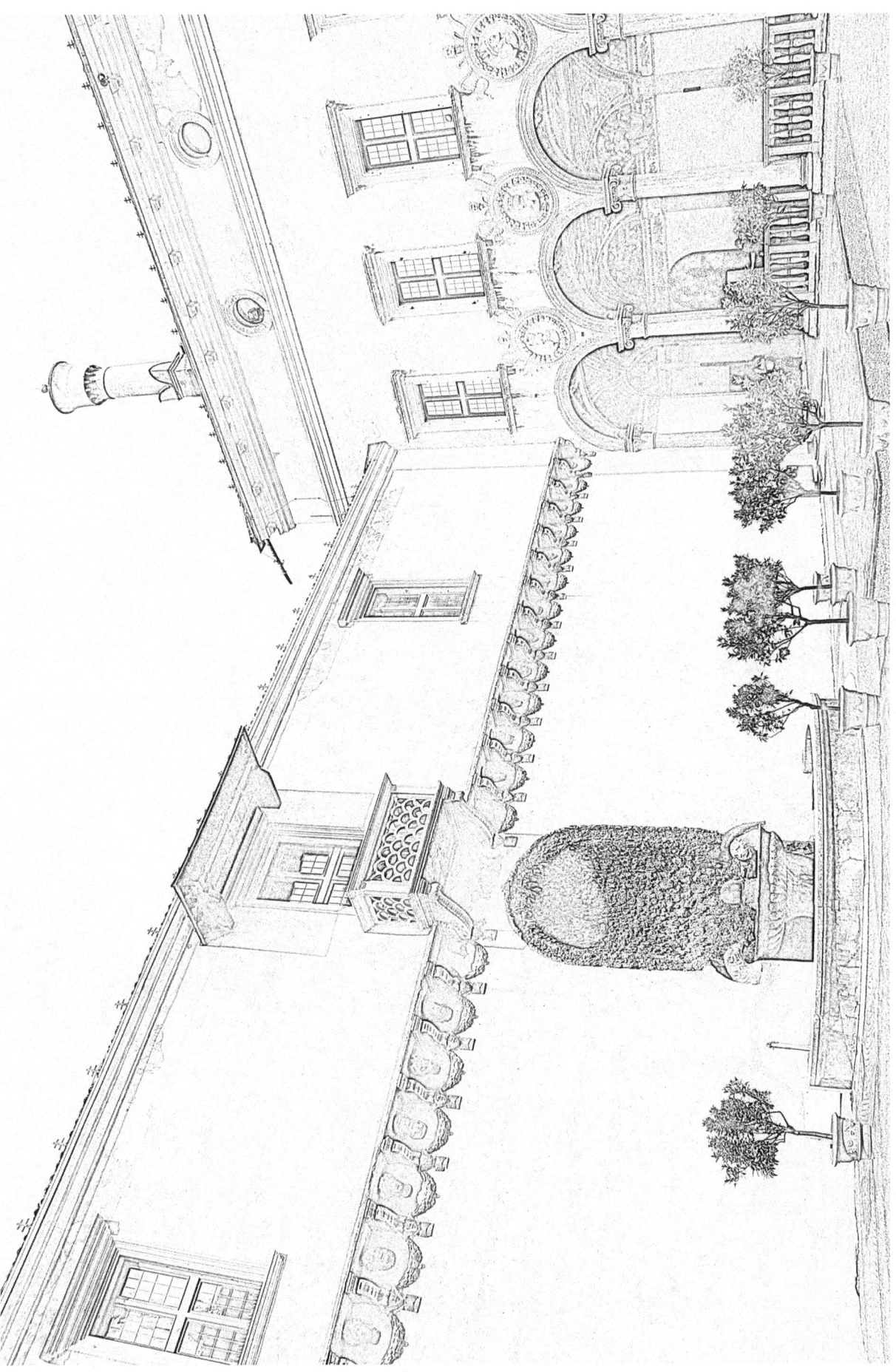

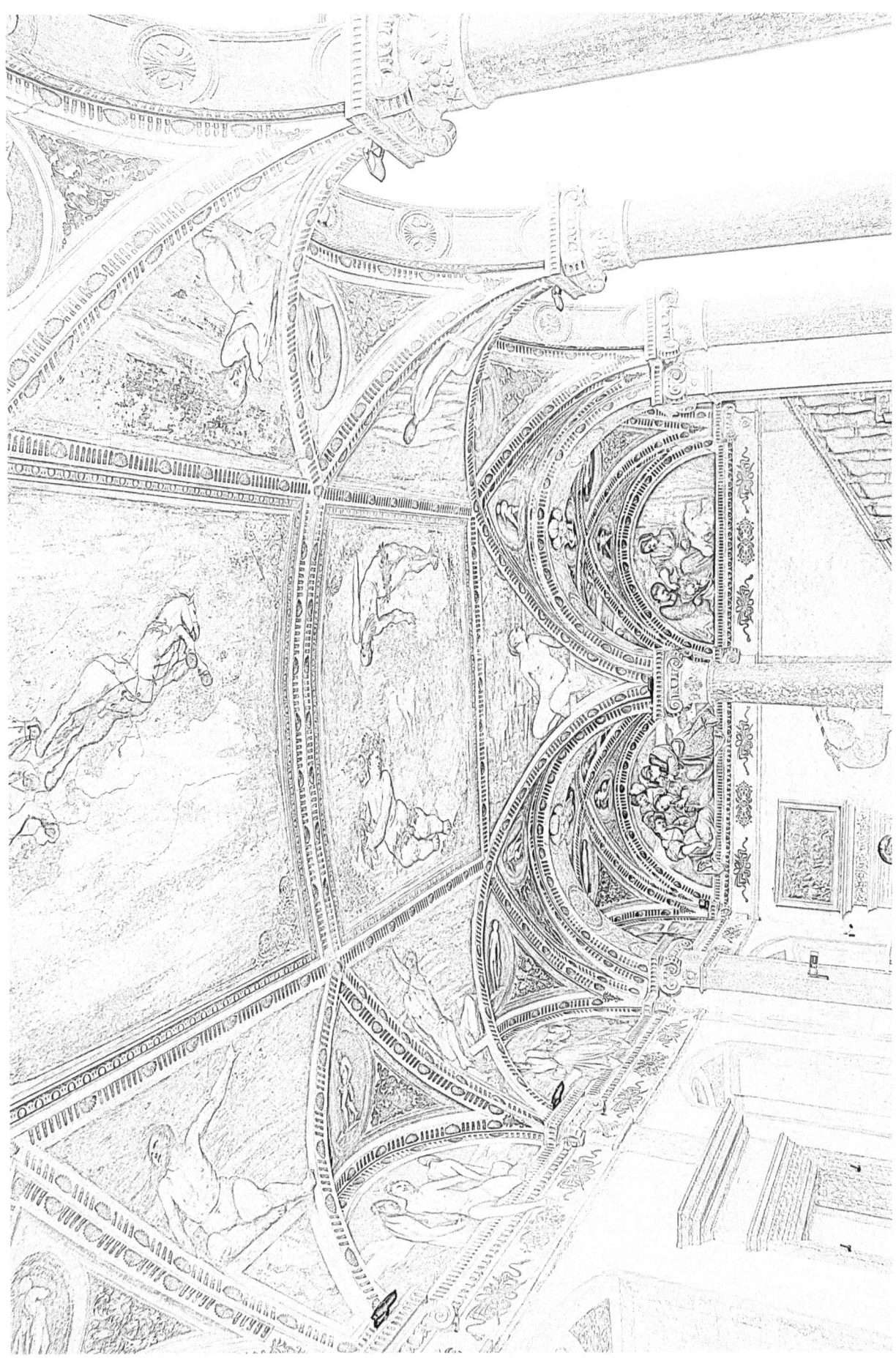

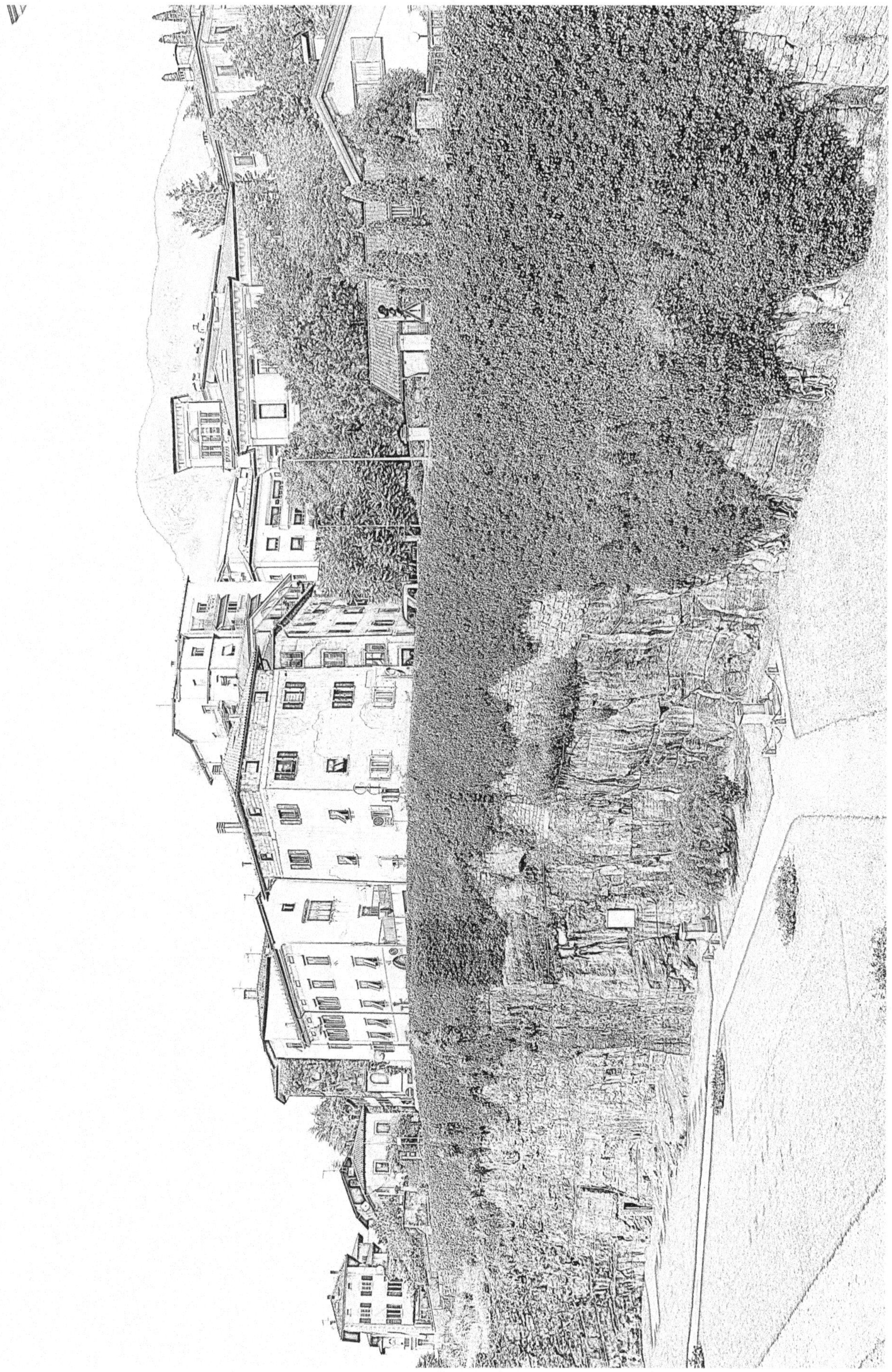

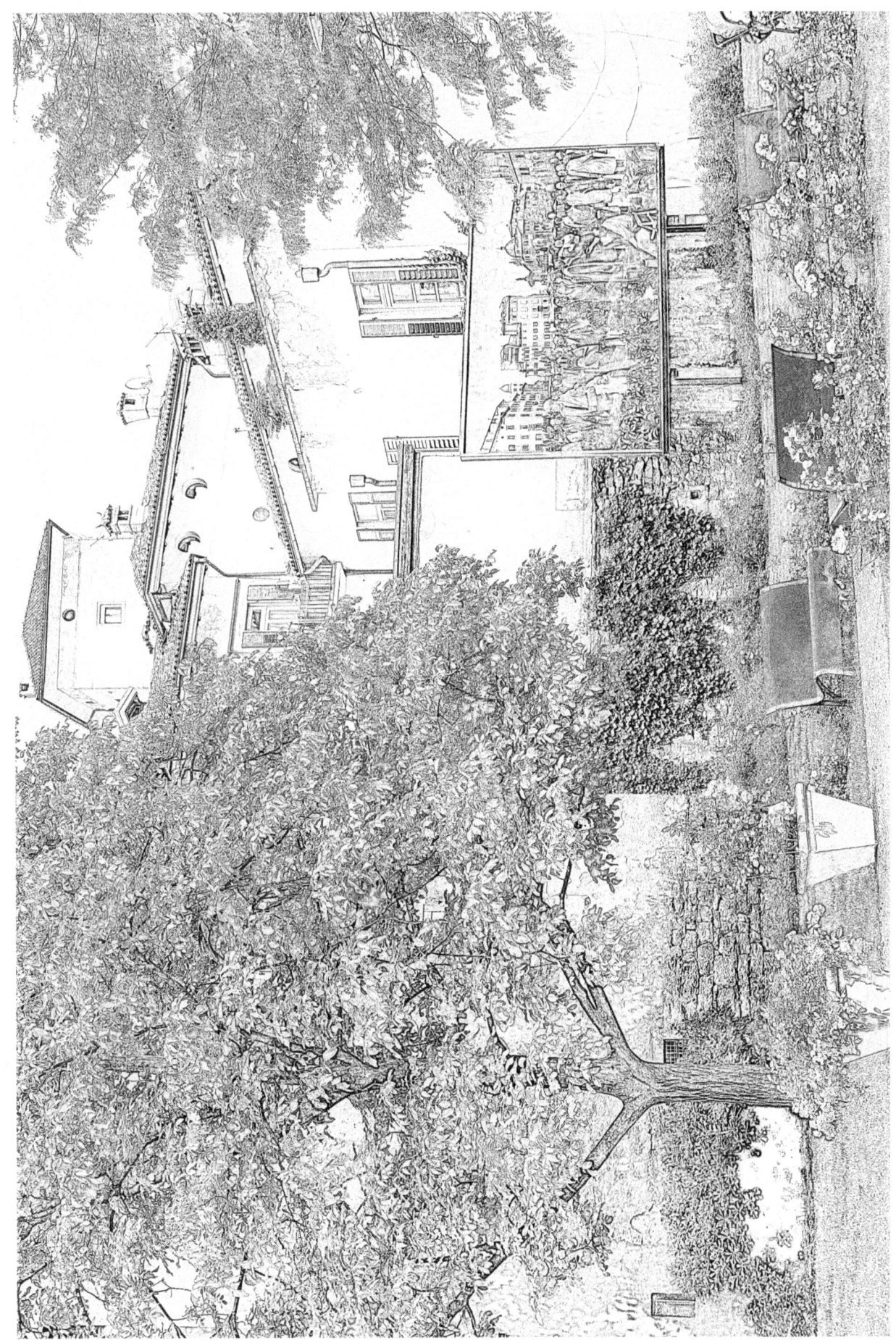

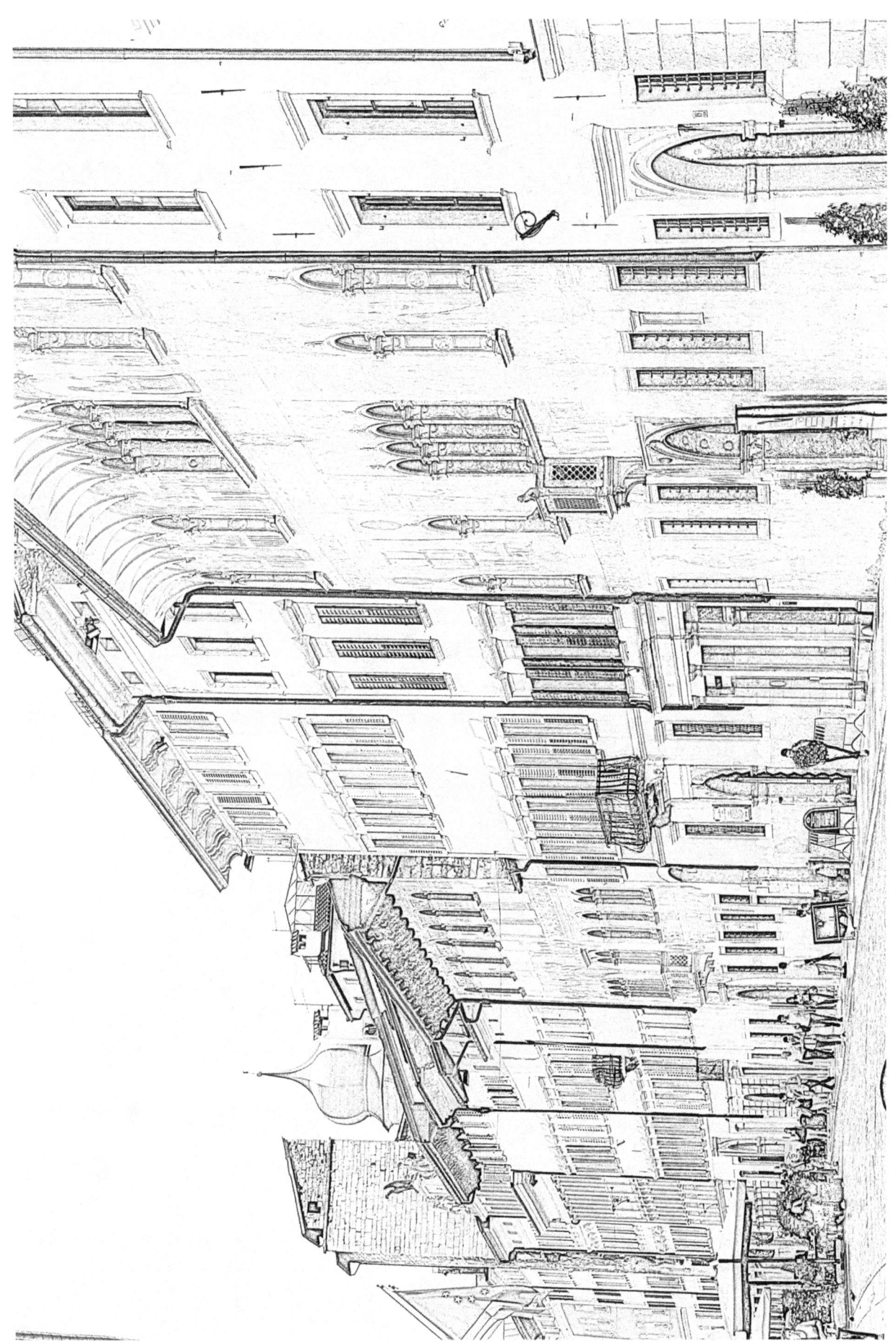

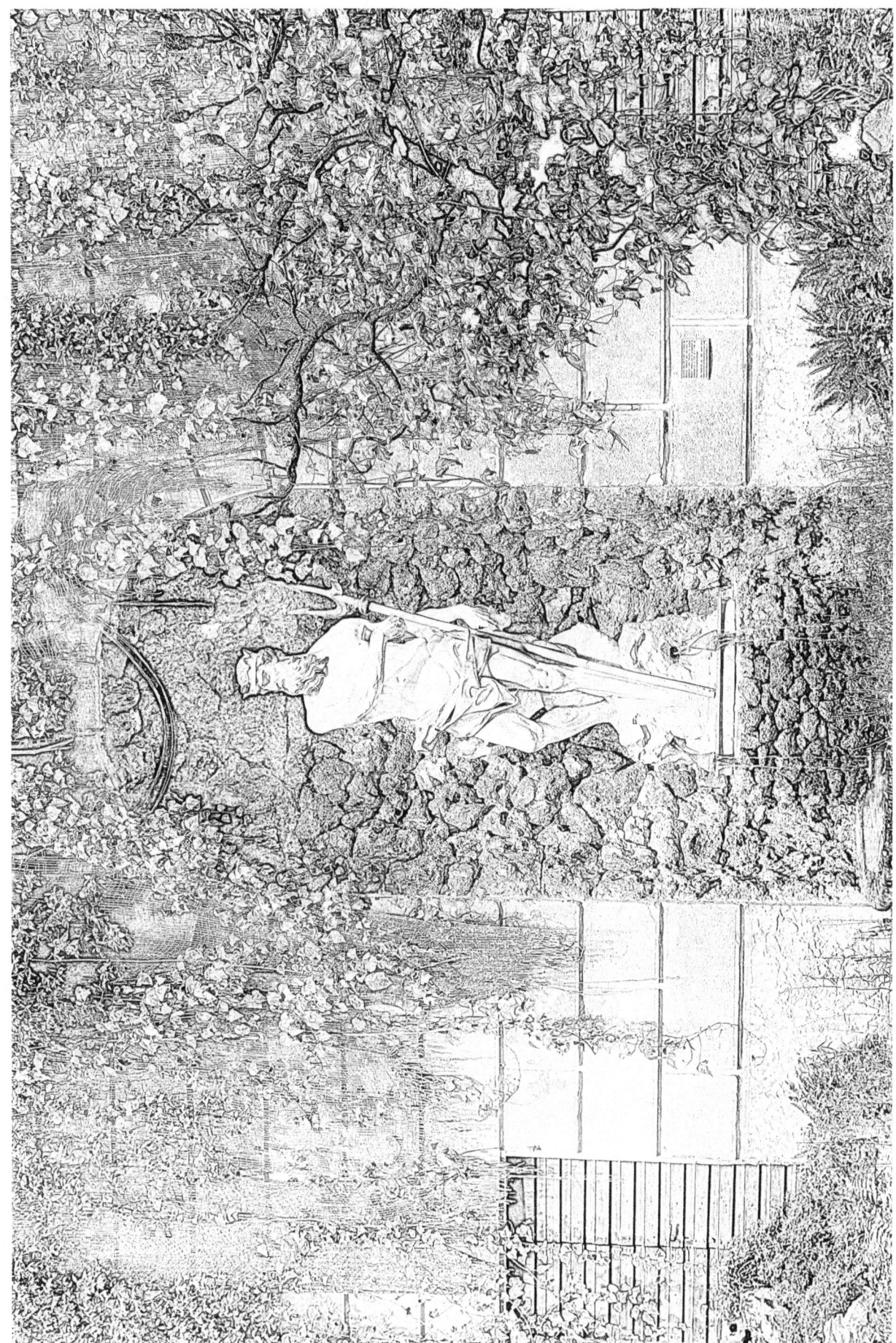

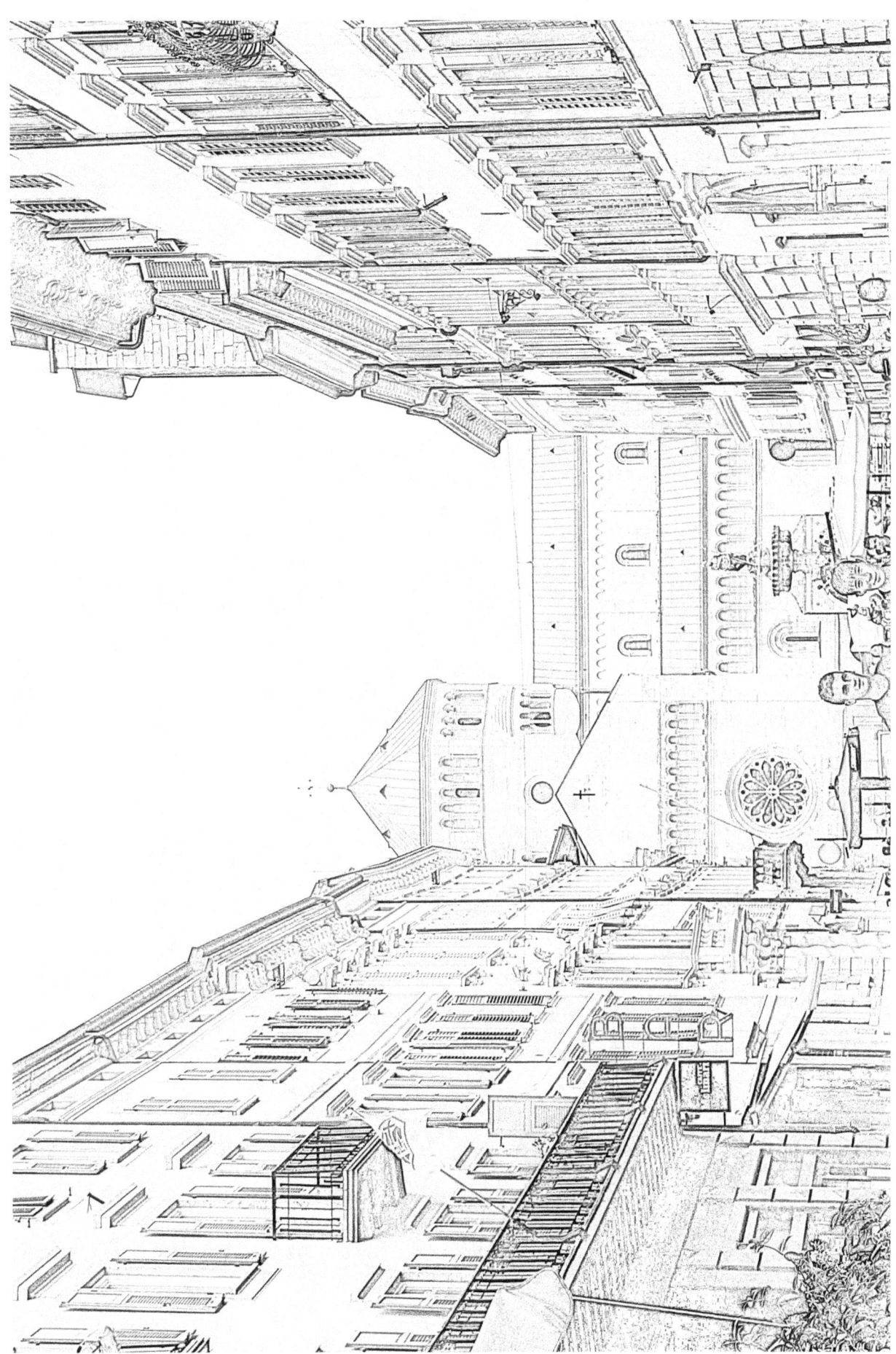

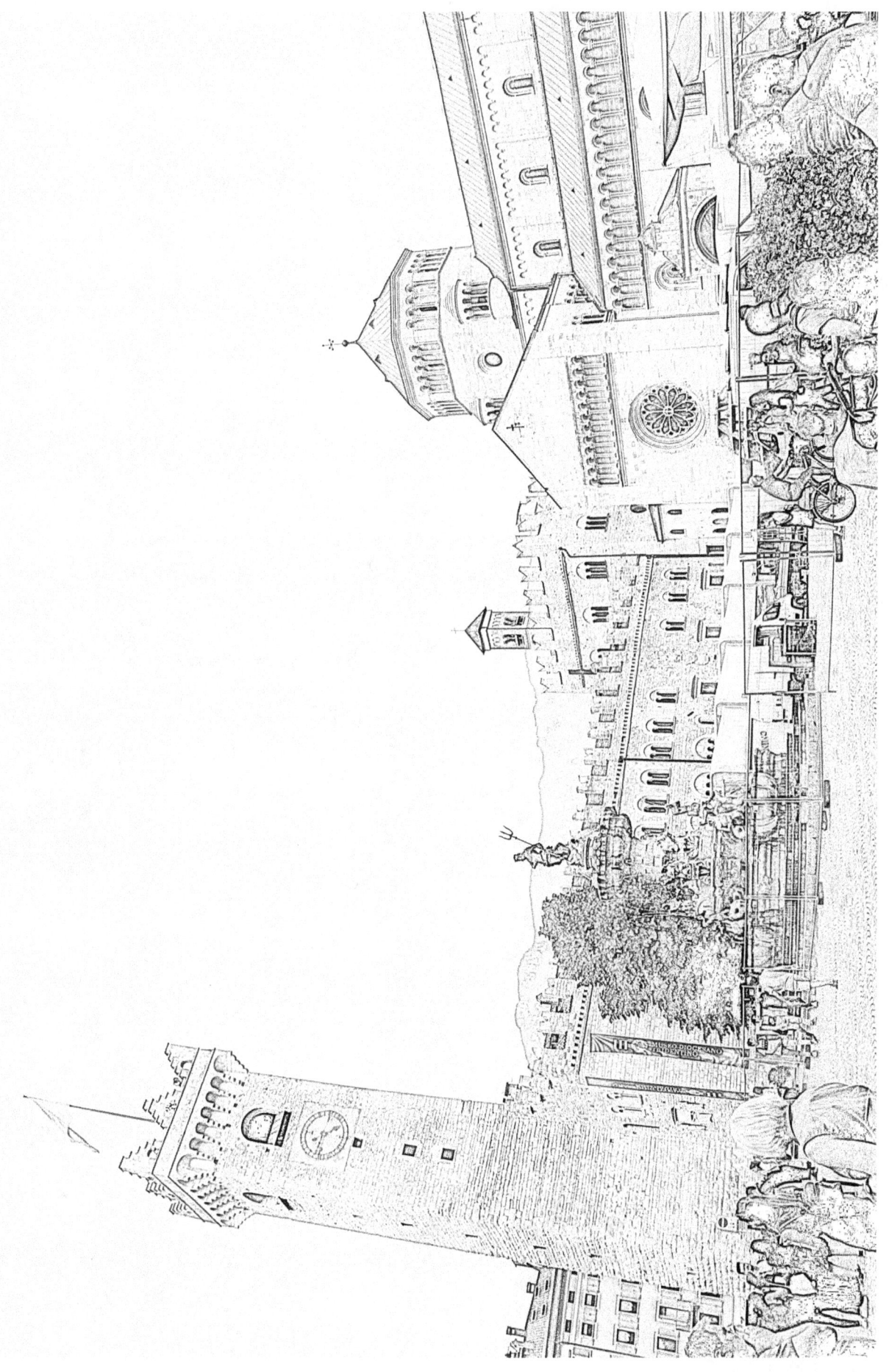

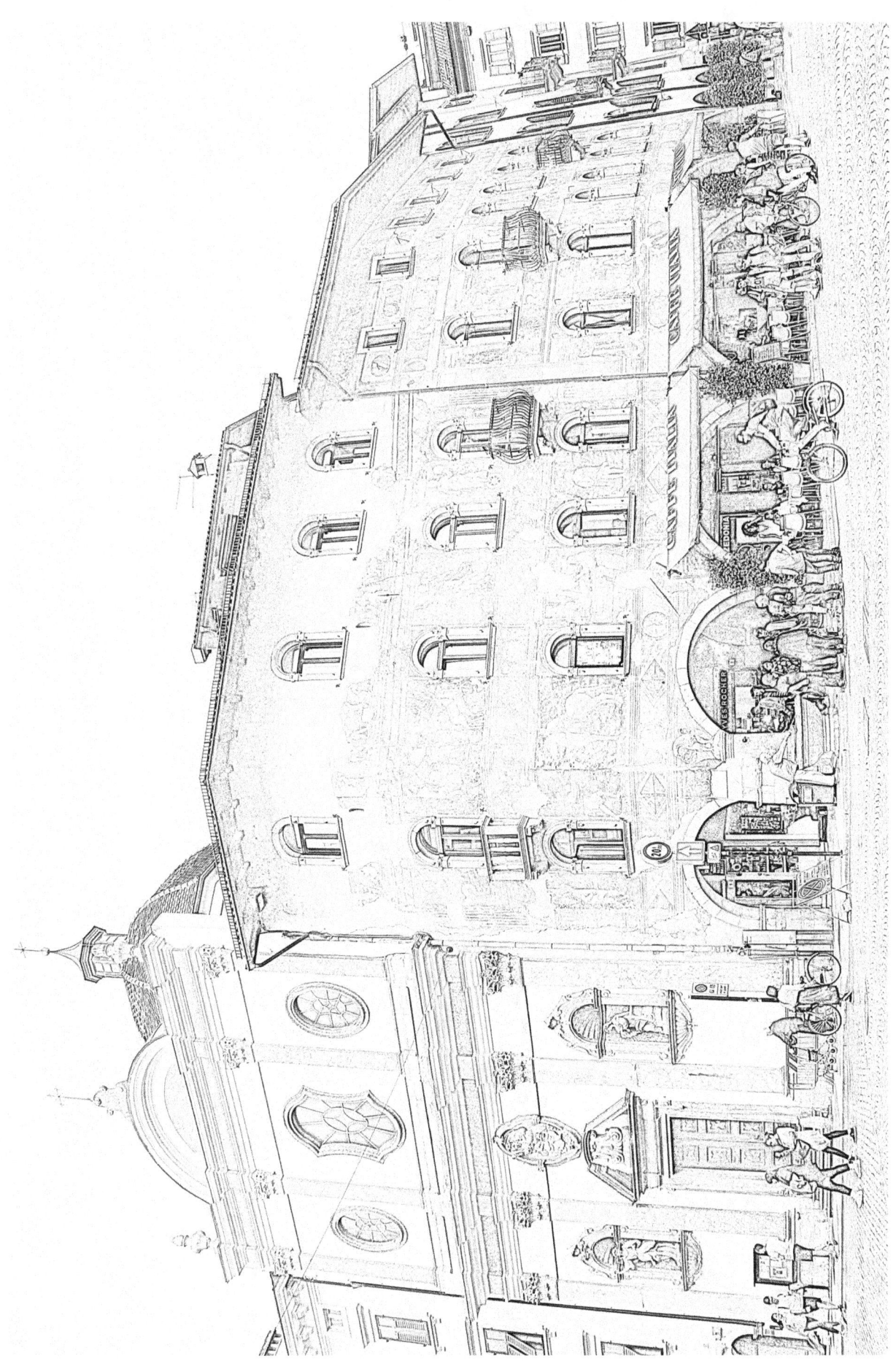

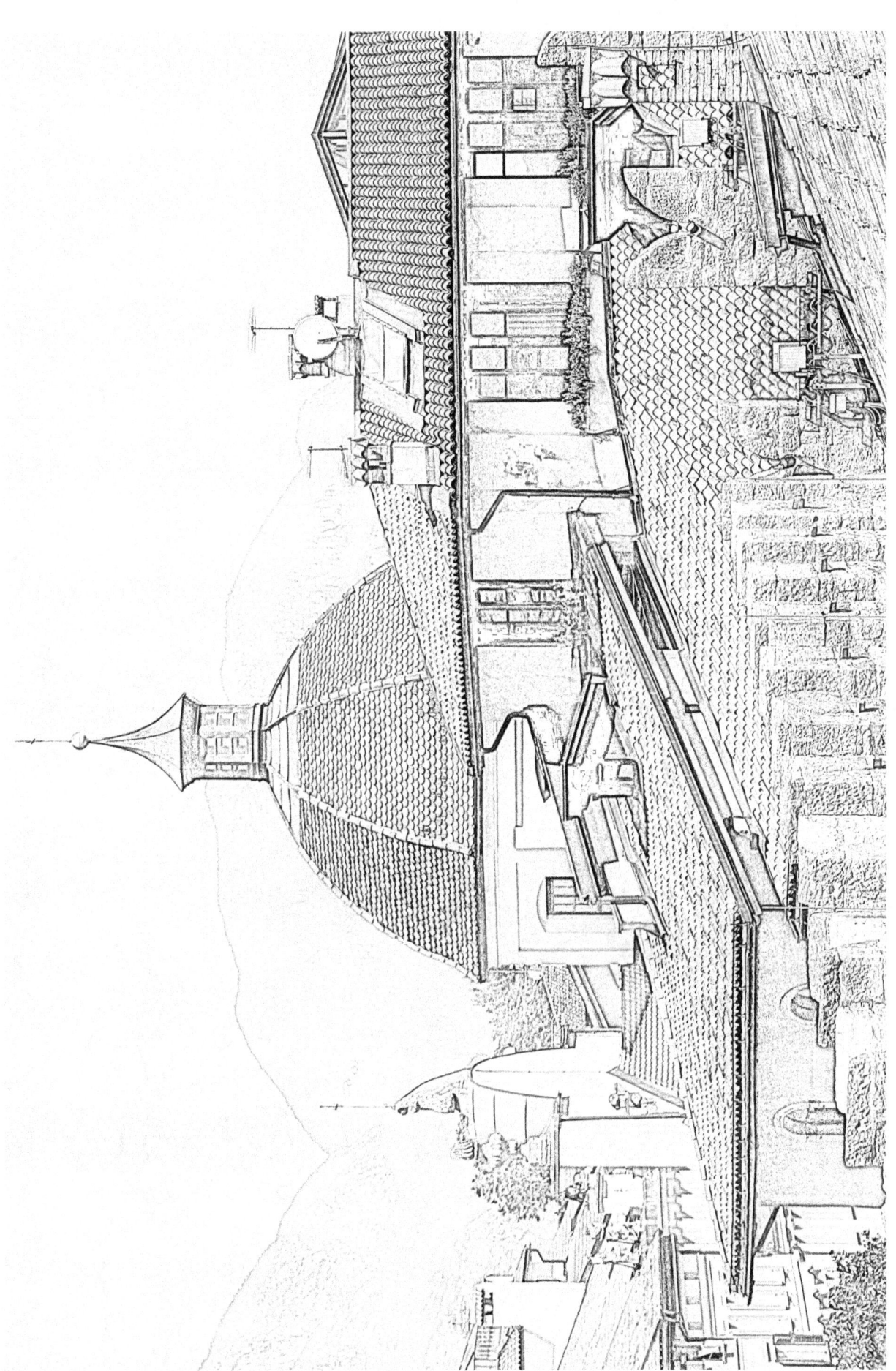

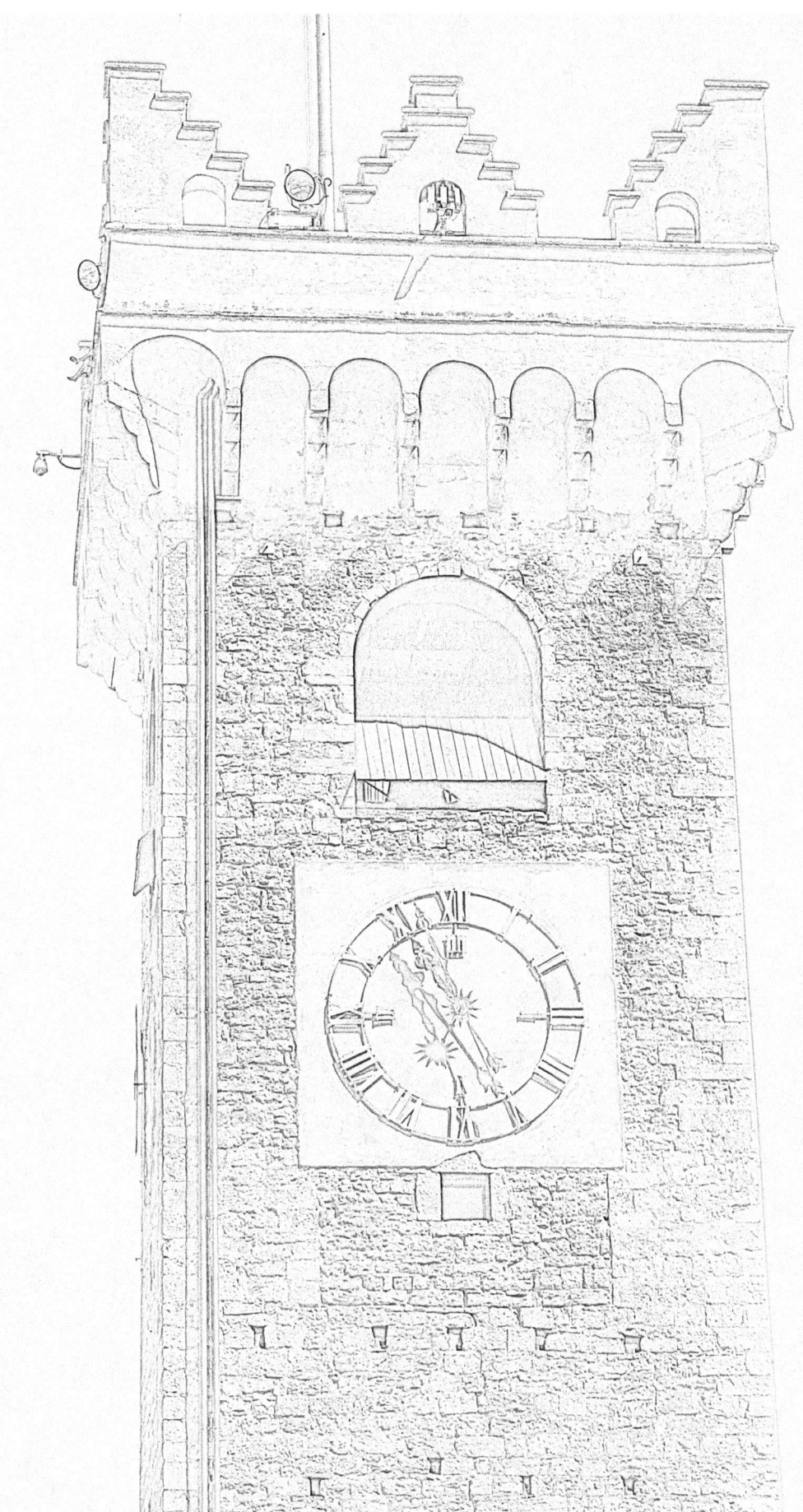

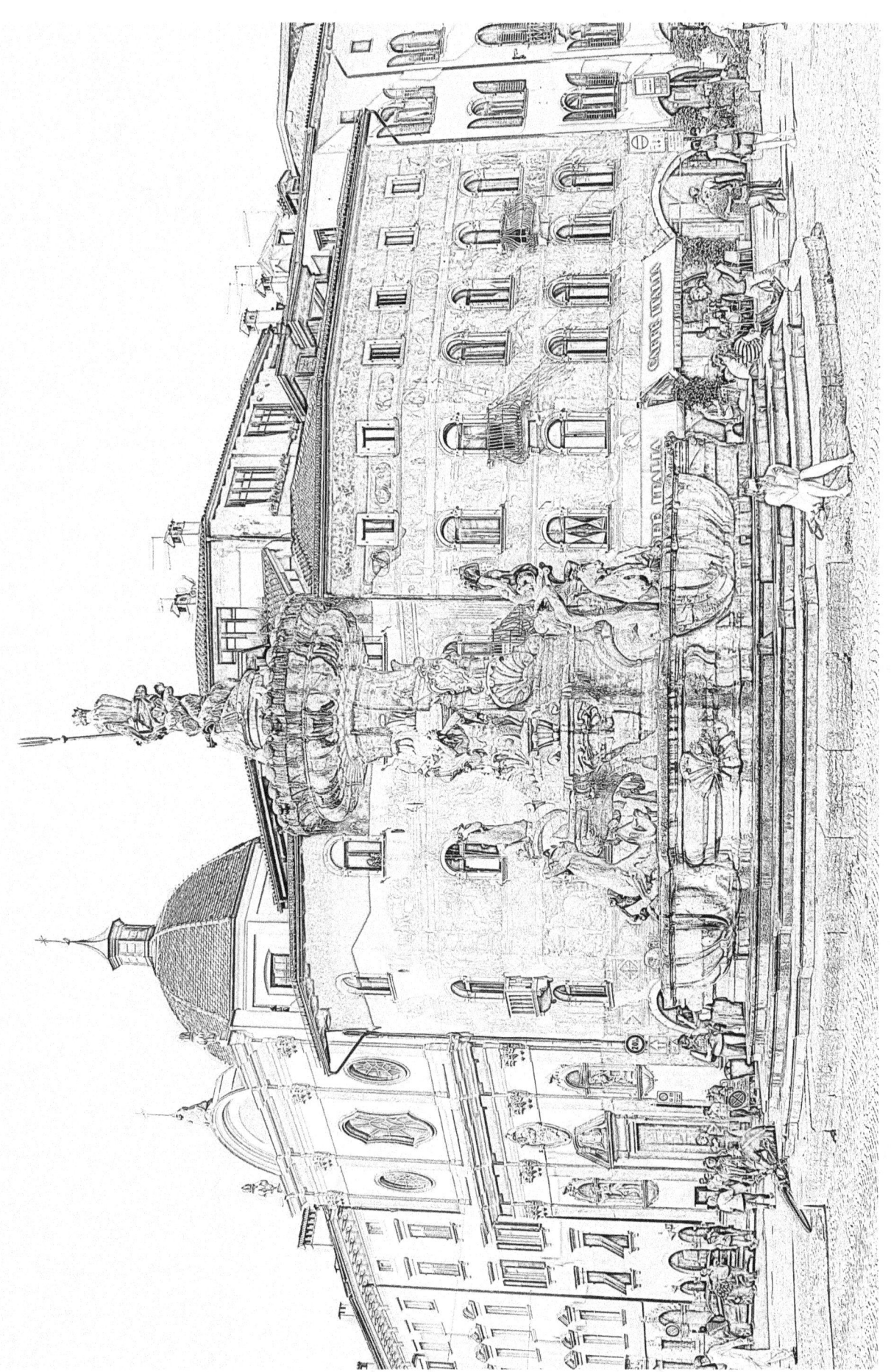

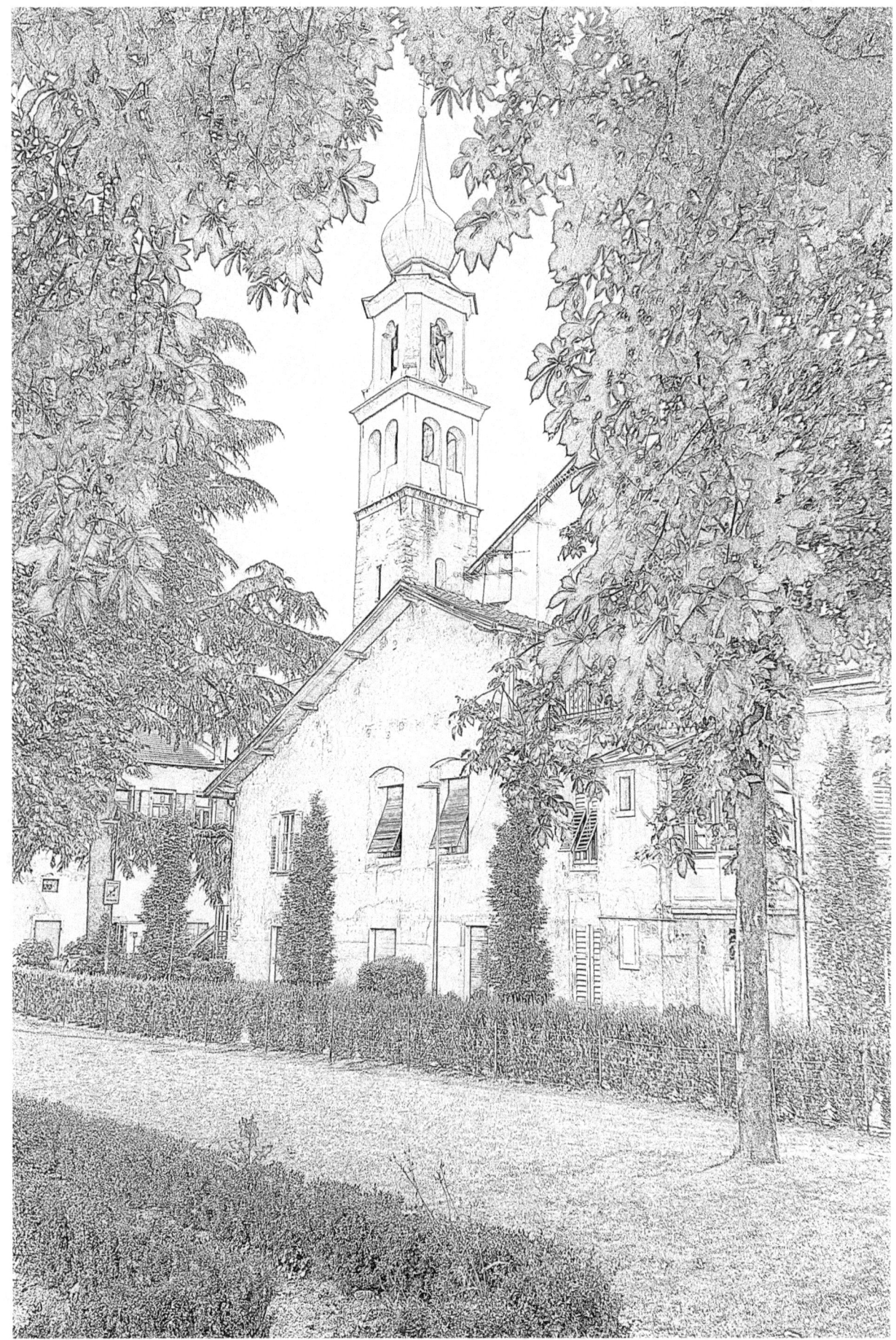

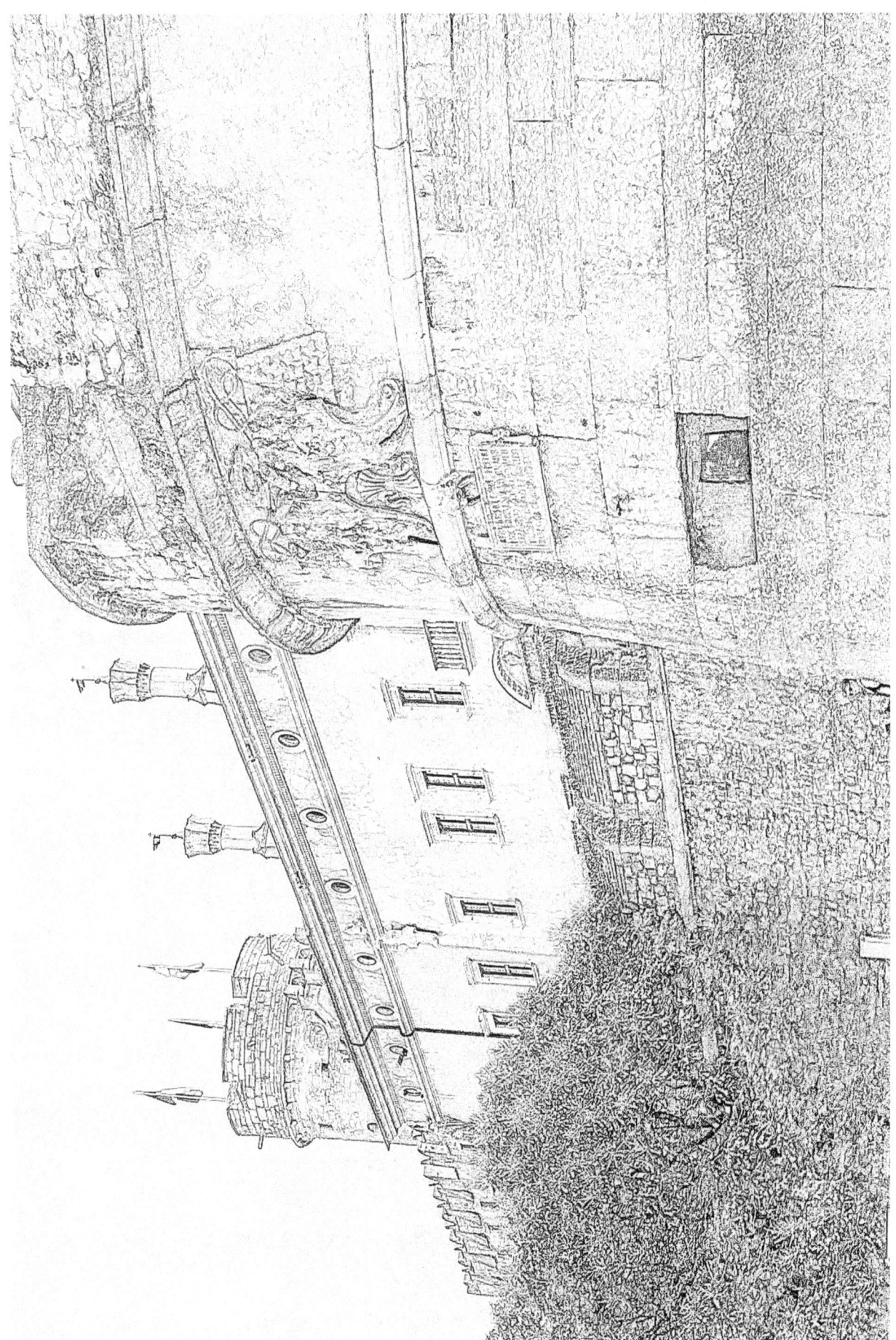

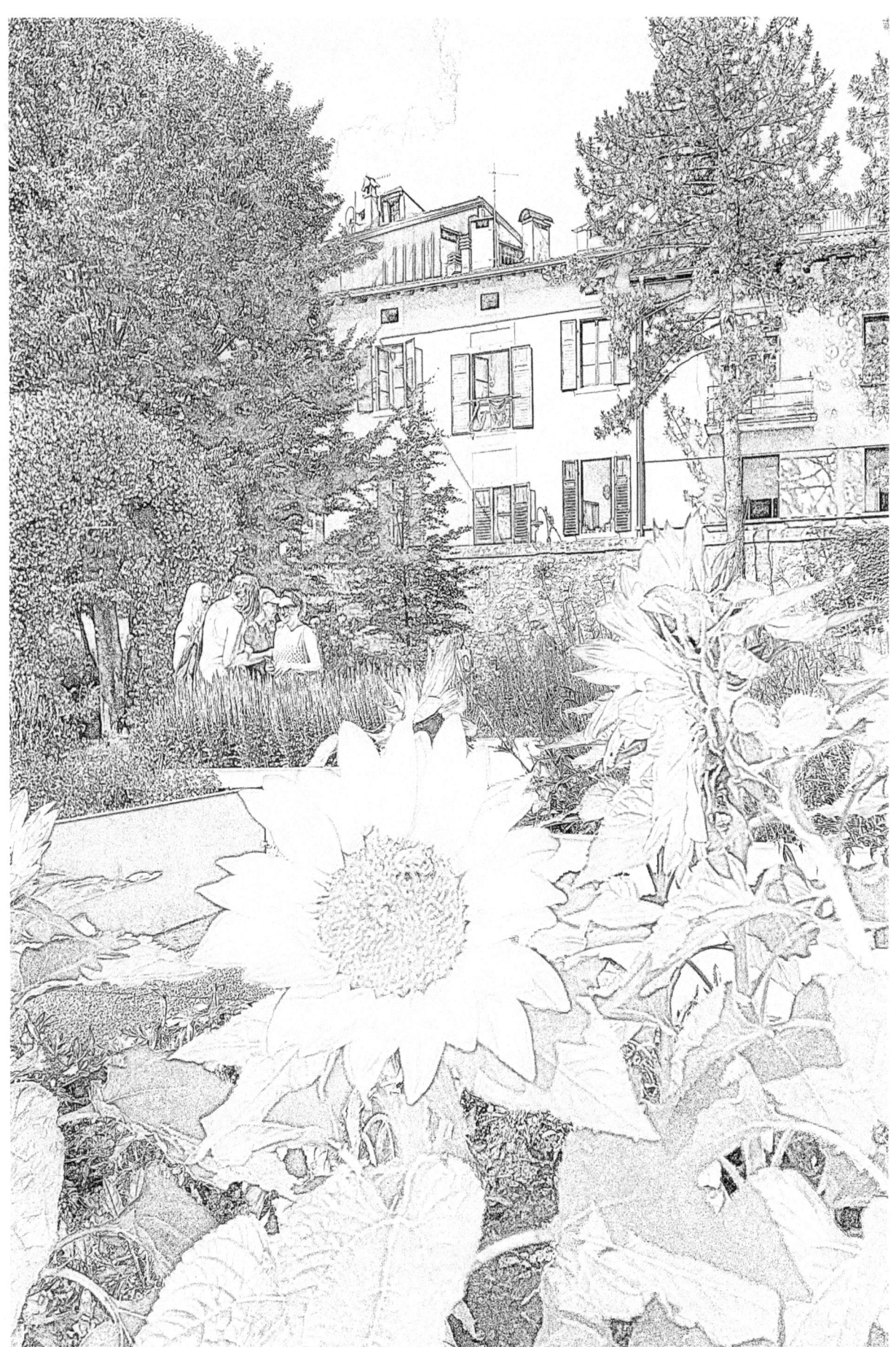

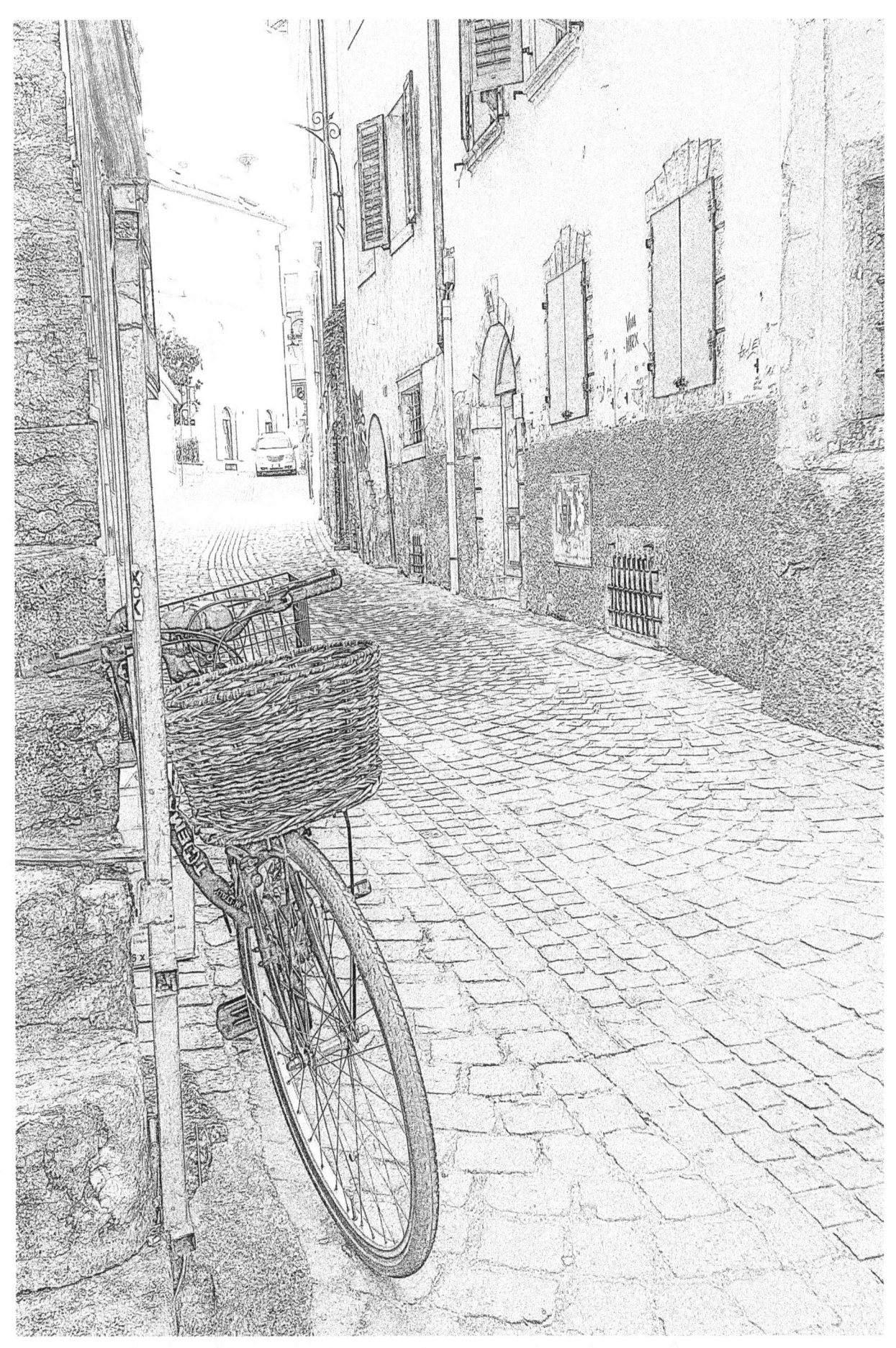

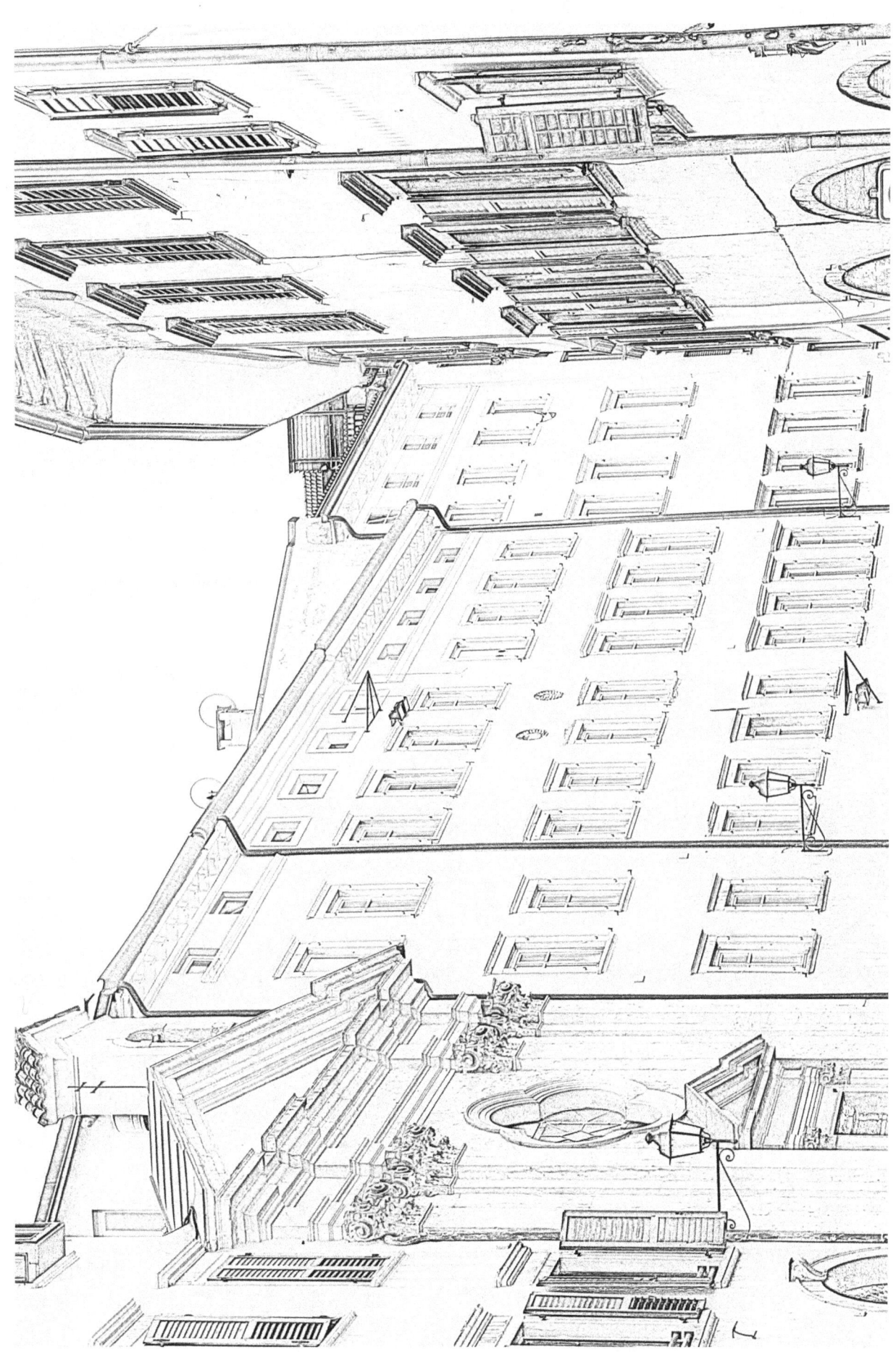

www.ingramcontent.com/pod-product-compliance
Lightning Source LLC
Chambersburg PA
CBHW080900170526
45158CB00016B/3073